D1472621

Cybernetics, Simulation, and Conflict Resolution

Cybernetics, Simulation, and Conflict Resolution

Proceedings of the
Third Annual Symposium
of the
American Society for Cybernetics

Edited by

Douglas E. Knight

Huntington W. Curtis

and

Lawrence J. Fogel

SPARTAN BOOKS

NEW YORK • WASHINGTON

Library of Congress Catalog Card Number 77-118150
International Standard Book Number 0-87671-165-4

Sole distributor in Great Britain, the British Commonwealth, and the Continent of Europe:

MACMILLAN & CO. LTD.
4 Little Essex Street
London, W. C. 2

Printed in the United States of America.

Cybernetics, Simulation, and Conflict Resolution

Dedication

Warren Sturgis McCulloch, poet, philosopher, logician, engineer, physician, neurophysiologist, neuropsychiatrist and cybernetician, was born on 16 November 1898. On 24 September 1969, after working on one of his papers at his farm in Old Lyme, Connecticut he went into bed early one morning, never to wake up. Heart failure was the cause.

Of course these dates are meaningless for Warren McCulloch—a mythical figure—extends into the remote past and as far into the future as there will be men who delight in the pleasures of a lively mind that desires, perceives, and thinks. He was there when Aristotle put his hand down to write the opening sentence to *Metaphysics*, "All men by nature desire to know"; when Shakespeare began to write the one hundred and eighth sonnet, "What's in the brain that ink may character/ Which hath not figur'd to thee my true spirit?"; when Leibnitz noted "I have here a number system to write all numbers that is only of 'zeros' and 'ones'; moreover, I found, this system contains the whole logic of dichotomies"; and he will be there and awake when Friars Bacon and Bungay's brass head speaks.

Warren McCulloch is a principle. He is the principle of doubting the apparently obvious and of sensing relations among apparent heterogeneities. This principle asks: "What is a number, that a man may know it, and a man that he may know a number?" Or "Where is fancy bred?" and it answers, "How we know universals" or "Why the mind is in the head." It is the principle that does not know of disciplinary boundaries; it is the principle that brings about the coincidentia oppositorum. The American Society for Cybernetics is a brainchild of this principle. Hence, the mythical figure, the principle, will be our guide. We dedicate this book to

WARREN S. McCULLOCH

HEINZ VON FOERSTER
University of Illinois
Urbana, Illinois

Contents

III. INTERNATIONAL CONFLICT ANALYSIS AND SIMULATION

IV. THE TECHNOLOGY: CYBERNETICS IN THE SEVENTIES AND BEYOND

The Participants

DR. HAYWARD R. ALKER, JR.*
Department of Political Science
Massachusetts Institute of Technology
Cambridge, Massachusetts

DR. MILTON U. CLAUSER
Director, Lincoln Laboratory and
Professor of Aeronautics
Massachusetts Institute of Technology
Cambridge, Massachusetts

DR. IVO K. FEIERABEND
Department of Political Science
San Diego State College
San Diego, California

DR. DAVID P. GARDNER
Vice Chancellor and
Associate Professor of Education
University of California at Santa Barbara
Santa Barbara, California

DR. I. J. GOOD
Department of Statistics and
Statistical Laboratory
Virginia Polytechnic Institute
Blacksburg, Virginia

DR. HERBERT GROSCH*
Director of the Center for
Computer Sciences and Technology
National Bureau of Standards
Gaithersburg, Maryland

DR. HAROLD GUETZKOW
Department of Political Science
Northwestern University
Evanston, Illinois

DR. CARL HAMMER
Director, Computer Sciences
UNIVAC Corporation
Washington, D.C.

DR. RICHARD D. LEVÉE
Staff General Manager,
Marketing Information Systems
Control Data Corporation
Minneapolis, Minnesota

DR. JOSEPH MOUNT
Manager, IBM Scientific Centers
IBM Corporation
White Plains, New York

DR. E. RAYMOND PLATIG
Director of the Office of External Research
U.S. Department of State
Washington, D.C.

DR. THOMAS C. SCHELLING
Center for International Affairs
Harvard University
Cambridge, Massachusetts

LT. COL. MERLE W. SCHOTANUS*
Joint Chiefs of Staff
Washington, D.C.

DR. MUZAFER SHERIF
Department of Sociology
Pennsylvania State University
University Park, Pennsylvania

DR. MARTIN SHUBIK
Department of Administrative Sciences
Yale University
New Haven, Connecticut

DR. RAYMOND TANTER
Department of Political Science
The University of Michigan
Ann Arbor, Michigan

DR. PRESTON VALIEN
Acting Associate Commissioner for Higher Education
Department of Health, Education, and Welfare
Washington, D.C.

DR. JOHN VOEVODSKY
Cybernetica Research Corporation
Stanford, California

DR. STANLEY WINKLER
Office of Emergency Preparedness
Executive Office of the President
Washington, D.C.

---

*Every symposium has its casualties. Dr. Richard Bellman of U.S.C. was sched-
uled to address the convention on the topic, "The Construction of Vignettes:
Short Simulation Processing for Role Playing Purposes." He cancelled out at
the last moment due to a conflict of schedule and a lack of suitable train con-
nections from the West Coast. (Dr. Bellman has an aversion to flying).

Dr. Haywood Alker of M.I.T. presented an excellent paper at the ASC conference but, unfortunately, he had made a previous commitment to have the
paper published elsewhere (in a journal he is editing). Any queries on Dr.
Alker's paper, "A Cybernetic Model of Peace-Seeking Activities in the International System," should be directed to him at M.I.T.

Lt. Col. Merle W. Schotanus, another of the participants not published in
these proceedings, presented a film on "Politico-Military Gaming." Queries
should be directed to Col. Schotanus at the Joint War Games Agency, Politico-
Military Division, Joint Chiefs of Staff, Washington, D.C.

Final speaker of the National Science Foundation supported symposium
was Dr. Herbert Grosch, then Director of the NBS Center for Computer Sciences. Dr. Grosch addressed a problem of major concern to today's tech-
nologists—central data banks and privacy.

The symposium was held within Dr. Grosch's own balliwick, The National
Bureau of Standards, and NBS personnel were responsible for recording all
of the presentations for subsequent use in developing these proceedings. Un-
fortunatly, due to a technical oversight unknown at the time, Dr. Grosch's
paper was the only one given from notes that was not recorded. The notes
were subsequently lost, making a realistic recreation unpractical. For this
reason, we regret that Dr. Grosch's full comments will not be included in this
proceedings.

Preface

It was Moratorium Day in Washington, D.C. Nearby, in the rolling hills of Gaithersburg, Maryland, at the steel-and-glass National Bureau of Standards building, an elite gathering of educators, government officials, computer scientists, and engineers met to interact on the problems of campus confrontation and conflict resolution.

As senior educators took to the conference podium to present their views of the problems on the nations campuses, the echoes of dissent resounded as distant thunder while student demonstrators began to gather for Moratorium Day observances at the White House, the Washington Monument, and the Justice Department—across the city, across the east coast, across the nation.

The motivation for the conference was to bring together the people with the problems and the people with the technology to see if somehow interaction between the two might suggest some useful courses of action. Several of the attendees were selected because of their experience in developing simulations of major social systems. Could the simulation laboratory offer a testing ground for developing possible alternatives to violence?

Time alone will reveal how successful were the hundreds of thousands who registered their discontent by marching, picketing, and standing their lonely vigils. Time also will reveal the success of the few hundreds who participated in the Third Annual Symposium of the American Society for Cybernetics. To a degree, their success can be measured in the proceedings, for their thoughts are recorded herein for history to measure. Although a proceedings by name and intent calls for the final product to be a close relative to the original report, in several instances our authors took advantage of their rewrite period to produce results which reflect some modifications in thought based on their interaction with the participants of the symposium.

From a positive viewpoint, the meeting brought together an extremely well motivated group of experts in the fields of education, government, and science. Educators defined their problem—the campus confrontation; statesmen defined theirs—international conflict resolution; and scientists presented a forward look at the technology of the seventies. The interaction that took place between the podium and the floor did not, perhaps could not, put a handle on solutions to the problems of "difference" we face today. Some of the Moratorium Day demonstrators offered simple solutions, but none of the speakers at the symposium did. The problems are large, forbidding, and too often seek violent solutions. They are local; they are international. Too often, solutions are too little, too late, too much, or too poorly motivated. Unfortunately, no one can define the solutions, much less apply them usefully. The result is Kent State, Vietnam, the Middle East, and South Africa.

An effective testing ground for viable solutions might be the simulation laboratory. When an aerodynamic engineer decides to flight test his new aircraft design in a computer simulator, he can expect to produce useful results. The physical characteristics of his materials are known, the physics of structures are well established, and his stress equations can be expected to produce viable data.

Not so with the social scientists. Unfortunately, as our speakers' presentations verified, simulation of human systems is still an imperfect science. The problems are large and complex, with subtle variables that are often unknown, often factors of chance. These are, to say the least, difficult parameters to develop. When the interactive forces are complex and infinite, how can they be synthesized?

When the "pieces" in a programmed simulation are moved,

they follow certain prescribed rules, as in computer chess. One knows the limits of each alternative. The game has rules that everyone follows. But in life, there are no defined limits on what the player can do. There may be laws, but our problems occur when laws—civil or international—are broken. That's tough to simulate. How can one program emotions? Or errors in judgment? Who would have believed a computer printout that predicted the weird judgments of Hitler in the closing days of World War II: military decisions based on astrological projections?

One factor limiting present simulations is the capacity of the files in existing computer systems. In the not too distant future (Dr. Joseph Mount predicts) storage capacity will no longer be a problem. Future ultraintelligent machines (UIMs as projected by Dr. Jack Good) may well (Dr. Carl Hammer proposes) gain their superior edge on man by approximating the central nervous system. Given a number of UIMs playing all of the human roles, could simulations of the world system ever be effective?

The answer may well be a qualified "yes," not just because of improving simulation techniques but also because man in the future years may become more regimented, thus more predictable, and therefore more easy to simulate. Today, with many options still available to individuals, man can be quite unpredictable when put into a stress situation.

Today, with the population explosion, we are forced increasingly to accept many restrictions. The more people come to interact with each other because of mushrooming population, the more rules and laws they require to live together, and the more conforming they become. Conformists should be more predictable. In many Communist countries brainwashing is becoming a very skillful tool for revising—even changing—men's minds. Whether the conformity of the future is brought about by highly sophisticated levels of brainwashing, programmed instruction, or genetic tampering, the future for at least half the world looks rather gloomy, but perhaps, more predictable. If man of the future does become more predictable, then simulation experts may finally become satisfied as improved computer programs and conformist man merge into a known future. A rather dismal prospect.

One wonders if perhaps the violence of today may be the final throes of the human species, kicking and fighting its way to a grave dug by its own machines. Overpopulation is driving us to machines to help control the monster networks needed for supplying the needs of civilized life. The question appears to be—will we be able to control the poplation problem before the machine gains too much control over us (before we become so dependent on the machine that there is no backing away)?

Some religious prophets have predicted that the year 2000 will presage 1000 years of peace. Dr. Jack Good calls for his UIM by 1994 ± 10—roughly by the same time. Perhaps the next evolutionary stage on this planet will spring from man's intellect rather than from his loins—perhaps the time is upon us.

DOUGLAS E. KNIGHT

Keynote Address

Conflict resolution is of obvious interest to all who find themselves in conflict. Unfortunately, in view of the nature of the industrial society which now dominates the world—a society built on economic competition—this includes nearly everyone. All too often competition leads to conflict and conflict leads to violence. The avoidance of conflict should be of even greater importance than the resolution of conflict, but has received far less attention.

We now stand at a unique point in history. The population explosion is coupled with a technological explosion, so that individuals and larger-scale social entities to which they belong impinge upon one another to an increasing extent. The more homogeneous they become, the more similar their goals, and thus, the greater the expected overlap of their goal-seeking activity. Competition for a finite resource is expected to result in mutual interference, resulting hostility, and possibly the kind of violence which may well be enormously magnified through the destructive use of technology.

Science is non-valuative, the intent being to gain a greater understanding of nature. Technology, a product of science, provides new means for the study of nature, including human behavior. It is entirely appropriate, therefore, that we turn our attention to how science and technology might best be used to avoid unnecessary violence. A comprehensive view of cybernetics provides the necessary platform for such an inquiry.

A number of hypotheses have been offered to account for human conflict. According to one, man is inherently warlike and responds to deep-seated instincts. Another points to the territorial imperative which demands that the homeland be defended from actual or presumed threats. Both these hypotheses now appear to be inappropriate.

Perhaps people need conflict in order to verify and perceive their group identity. Perhaps the very structure of society generates situations which force individuals and larger-scale social entities into conflict, which can be resolved only through violence. Clearly, this subject is of great importance to us all. It deserves scientific investigation and the use of whatever technology can be brought to bear to provide greater insight and alternative courses of action toward conflict resolution. Presumably there are alternative ways to purchase freedom, at less cost in terms of violence, than have yet been found.

Cybernetics provides the interdisciplinary scope and principles which are appropriate for addressing this problem area, since conflict is a particular form of communication and thus, arises from closed-loop processes. Each participant within the conflict models himself and his opponents in the light of presumed goals. Hopefully, improved modeling might avoid fruitless combat by revealing higher-level goals of all participants which overlap to an extent sufficient to elicit their cooperation in place of continued lower-level conflict. Many questions remain to be answered: How specific should statements of goal be in various situations? What are appropriate means for representing the hierarchical structure of social entities as their behavior simultaneously affects multiple levels of interest? How precise should estimates be of the presumed goals of opponents in view of their observed behavior? Under what conditions is it well to introduce new players in the game in order to encourage greater objectivity on the part of the primary participants? Can the responsibility for unnecessary violence be affixed to insufficiency of sensory capability, to inadequacy of decision-making, and/or to improper control of overt responses?

The following papers examine only particular kinds of conflict. They consider various aspects of campus confrontation which illustrates conflict near at hand and readily observed by the academic community. They examine large-scale systems in conflict—the international scene as seen from an objective point of view. The symposium closed with a look ahead to cybernetics in the seventies—an examination of new technology and viewpoints which might be available within the coming decade. We were honored to have outstanding speakers, individuals who brought a wealth of information and worthwhile perspectives to these important topics.

Twenty-one years ago Norbert Weiner defined cybernetics as "communication and control in man and machine." He went on to call attention to the dangers in the misuse of technology and appealed for the "human use of human beings." In a very real sense, he is the one who called this symposium to order. His spirit of good will and intellectual inquiry will remain with us so long as we are concerned with this pervasive problem—the avoidance of unnecessary violence.

It was my privilege to be among those who participated in this event in the "coming of age" of cybernetics.

L. J. FOGEL

I
A Problem:
Campus Confrontation

Must We Change
for Change's Sake?

PRESTON VALIEN

Department of Health, Education, and Welfare
Washington, D. C.

A few weeks ago, during a coffee break at an academic conference, I happened to overhear three participants commiserating with each other on the ever-popular issue of student unrest. I had an unmistakable feeling of having been there before when I heard one of them protest, "Of course I'm not against needed change, but these kids seem to want change for change's sake."

We all want change when it is needed. The problem, of course, is that each of us defines "need" in terms of his own private vision of the ideal. The baffled professor—whose values and style were shaped in another milieu—surely wanted his students to enjoy a productive and satisfying life. But he was unable to grasp that a rapidly changing environment had helped to shape visions in them of the ideal which were vastly different from his own.

Change, of course, has always been part of the human condition; Heraclitus was teaching that all is flux in the fifth century B.C. What is different now is its sharply accelerating pace—particularly in the technological and social spheres—and the prospect that it will continue to come faster and faster into the indefinite future. The most important thing that is new, said the late Robert Oppenheimer,

3

. . . is the prevalance of newness. The changing scale and scope of change itself, so that the world alters as we walk in it, so that the years of man's life measure not some small growth or rearrangement of moderation of what he learned in childhood, but a great upheaval.

Under such conditions, it is small wonder that the authority of age is no longer undisputed, that long experience does not seem to count the way it used to. Indeed, things have come to such a pass—at least according to one prominent social psychologist—that today's parents, who can no longer even establish a range of alternative outcomes for their children's future, are useless and obsolete in a way that rarely befell parents of any previous century. To those of us who are parents, this must seem an excessively cruel judgment; yet most of us will at least secretly admit that we *are* beginning to doubt our own capacities for understanding the world in which our children live.

I am reminded of a recent cartoon in one of the national magazines depicting a frightened, potbellied, middle-aged man being dragged into a torch lit dungeon by a group of stern-looking members of the *Now* generation. As he disappears from view, the man is pathetically protesting, "But I *am* relevant, I tell you . . . relevant."

This is the kind of desperate feeling many of us have come to know too well. And because the healthy human mind must ultimately reject the idea of its own uselessness, we are prone to develop theories capable of reassuring ourselves that we are relevant after all—that it is the young who, for a variety of easily explained psychological reasons, are blinded to the true nature of reality. We devour with gusto 500-page tomes on the historical conflict between impulsive, complex-ridden youth and their forebearing fathers. We blame the permissiveness of Dr. Spock for creating a generation of tantrum-prone students who demand instant gratification of every wish. We bemoan the decline of reasoned discourse, and in the process we find some temporary balm for our troubled spirit.

"If the changes that we fear be irresistible," asked Samuel Johnson, "what remains, but to acquiesce with silence? It remains that we retard what we cannot repel, that we palliate what we cannot cure."

Perhaps there is considerable truth in the psychological-historical theories of student unrest. But if, in the interest of our own spiritual well being, we use them to rationalize a comforting belief in a world that no longer exists, we are inviting catastrophe for old and young alike. One does not need to swallow whole the esoteric theories of Marshall McLuhan to recognize that the brightest children of the first television generation would find the forms and content of a centuries-old academic system to be unbearably confining.

In truth, it is by now abundantly clear that *all* the major institutions of our society—for the most part designed to operate in extended periods of relative stability—have been incapable of responding to rapidly changing external realities. If the society is to avoid the catastrophic consequences of intergroup conflict, if it is to cope with the unforeseen environmental effects of our exploding technology, we must move to redefine the role of our outworn institutions.

It will not be enough to exchange one set of rigidities for others which are presumably more relevant in the year 1969. The task is to create institutions which can redefine their missions on a continuous basis to cope with the social and technological change which will increase *at an increasing rate.*

Paradoxically, the most potentially useful instrument society possesses for re-creating its basic institutions is itself an institution—one which is at present as rigid and out of date as any of the rest. During the 1970's we must redefine the role of our educational system to make it effective in producing the kind of human being who—in his own role as worker, parent, and citizen—can help the society to successfully cope with a constantly evolving future.

But how can we possibly begin to reform the educational system of an entire nation? Responsibilities for education in the United States are divided among state, federal, and local governments on the one hand, and private organizations on the other. The unique federal role is derived from its ability to view education from a national perspective. The Office of Education can first, *identify* those areas where change is needed to conform with new environmental realities; next, *develop* alternative approaches in educational structure, process, or content to meet the identified needs; and lastly, *provide* the information and financial resources required by the decentralized educational system for actual implementation. The process has two important features: *continuity*—that is, each identified need leads to the development and ultimate implementation of innovations in educational structure, process, or content; and *repetition*—that is, the cycle is repeated endlessly as the changing environment creates new educational needs.

Consider in this context the issues recently raised by a Health, Education and Welfare study group on the causes of educational tensions. This group was one of several set up by Secretary Robert Finch soon after he was appointed to delve deeply into the needs of American education in the coming decade. Its members spent much of last spring interviewing students, teachers, school administrators, local government officials, law enforcement officers, psychologists, and sociologists. They concluded that the issues underlying much of student protest in 1969 fall into four major categories, each of which relates intimately to the others. They are

1. dehumanization of society
2. inequitable distribution of wealth, power, and prestige
3. social and cultural exclusion
4. educational irrelevance.

Let's assume that widespread student concern in these areas is a reasonably good indication that our societal institutions are out of step with a changing environment. The question then arises: how can the educational system act to ameliorate the very real problems our students have identified? Let's take as an example the issue of dehumanization.

No matter what our age or position in the society we can probably recognize in ourselves the innermost feelings of the student who carries a picket sign reading "I am a human being. Please do not fold, spindle, or mutilate." The highly mechanized and automated techniques which have brought us an unprecedented level of material prosperity have exacted a heavy toll on the human spirit. Our institutions in this complex age of technology have begun to grow beyond the control or influence of any private persons and to take on a life of their own. Uncontrolled, they tend to become ends in themselves, grinding up individual human beings in the interest of self-perpetuation.

Nowhere is the dehumanizing process more apparent than in what has come to be known as the multiversity. If higher education is to become an instrument for remolding other major societal institutions in the image of responsive human service, it must first remold itself. Colleges and universities need to encourage a feeling of personal involvement, self-respect, and concern for others among their students. To meet this kind of challenge, forward-looking institutions all over the country are beginning to experiment with radical departures in academic structures and processes which have endured for generations.

They are beginning to "hang loose," for example, in such sacrosanct areas as admissions. We are finally beginning to realize that our nation is basically a pluralistic one, that vast numbers of poor black, brown, and red Americans have been denied the opportunity for human growth represented by higher learning, and that, as a result of this denial, students of all colors have missed a crucial, humanizing educational experience. The drive to reform obsolete standards of admission must be continued. Concurrently, colleges are duty bound to provide previously excluded students with financing, services, and curriculum appropriate to their needs.

One such needed service is ethnic studies. As more and more minority students gain admission to predominantly white campuses, they are expressing the need for a learning experience related to the uniqueness of their own cultural heritage. The social and cultural groups to which they belong were never assimilated into the larger society of nineteenth- and twentieth-century America; for them, the fabled melting pot was simply a convenient illusion of the dominant culture. But today the young people of all the historically repressed minori-

ties are affirming the validity of their heritage, and in the
process, they are rekindling the spark of human dignity that
centuries of majority rejection very nearly had extinguished.
It is a mark of the changing times that the minority struggle
for ethnic identity is receiving ever-increasing sympathy and
support from those contemporary white students who are
seeking new values appropriate to the latter part of the twentieth century.

I believe that this trend toward a new kind of cultural
pluralism embodying ethnic pride, mutual respect, and an
ultimate sharing of basic human values augurs well for the
future of our society. In any case the social forces already
bringing it into being are so powerful that debate over the
normative question of *desirability* is likely to prove largely
academic. American higher education must accept pluralism
as an emerging fact and proceed to define its own role in
easing the widespread disorientation which always accompanies
a transition from the old to the new.

Another crucial area of experimentation in the rehumanizing
of higher education involves the question of student participation—in curriculum development, institutional governance,
personal academic planning, and many other aspects of university life. The student of the new decade is a far cry from
the goldfish-swallowing, panty-raiding adolescent of earlier
generations. Young people are maturing today at an earlier
age than ever before, yet the demands of our increasingly
technical economy require that they spend a longer and longer
period in semidependent student status before assuming a role
in the mainstream of society.

Students have already shown themselves to be informed,
concerned, and generally responsible critics of the educational
system through their work in community action and campus
educational reform. They are in many ways more quickly and
deeply affected by the changing environment than the rest of
us, and for that reason alone they represent an invaluable
resource in the making of institutional—indeed national—policy.

At the root of campus tension is a deep disagreement about

the very nature of higher education. This generation of students questions whether the prevailing concept of college as a vocational training ground is wholly relevant in an age of profound social upheaval. Many of them feel the need to become actively involved in the great questions of the day, to break down the barriers which have separated man from man, and, in the process, to discover for themselves just what it is to be human. For these young people, the college years must provide an education that goes far beyond preparation for a lifetime vocation. They want to use this fleeting time to engage in a process of self-discovery that will prepare them to live as whole human beings in an age of increasing complexity.

Against these deeply felt convictions there generally stands a relatively inflexible institutional structure oriented toward the traditional, compartmentalized, dryly academic approach to learning. It is not surprising that the dammed-up frustration of the young sometimes finds release in unproductive confrontation. More often, however, students have channeled their energies into volunteer social and educational action projects of their own design. Uncounted thousands of young people are trying to increase their understanding of a changing world through tutoring disadvantaged children in the inner city, investigating the pollution of our physical environment, promoting the interests of the forgotten consumer, and creating the imaginative educational techniques typified by the free university movement.

A few courageous institutions have taken the students' cue and plunged into a totally new kind of learning environment. Rejecting piecemeal approaches to academic reform, they are attempting to construct from scratch a new kind of institution more responsive to the needs of the modern world. According to the announcement brochure for Johnston College, an experimental unit of the University of Redlands, California, "The touchstone for decision-making will be this question: What will most effectively promote the personal and social growth of the individual?" The new college will be designed to overcome rigidity in attitude and structure. It will eliminate traditional departmental boundaries in the interest of producing whole individuals who can involve themselves in solving complex societal problems. It will encourage a new kind of honesty and rapport between faculty and students—partly through the use of encounter techniques—all in the interest of enhancing the learning experience for both. Most important, it will emphasize self-directed study.

I have briefly mentioned several areas of academic reform—equal opportunity, ethnic studies, student participation, experiential (as opposed to classroom) education, new teacher-student relationships—all of which relate to the problem posed by a dehumanized society. It is characteristic of our interdependent age that reforms designed to attack this major problem will also help to bring about solutions to the other three issues identified by the HEW task force as sources of student unrest: inequitable distribution of wealth, power, prestige; social and cultural exclusion; and educational irrelevance.

Most of our institutions cannot, indeed should not, abandon hundreds of years of tradition overnight. There is an alternative to instant change on the one hand, and no change at all on the other. This "middle path" is being adopted by hundreds of colleges and universities all over the country as they begin to experiment on a piecemeal basis with new ways of doing business. In many cases these efforts have grown out of projects generated by the students themselves. Some of the new approaches are directed outward from the university, toward involvement with the pressing problems of the larger community. Others are probing into the internal affairs of the university itself in the search for a more meaningful educational experience. Whatever the emphasis of a specific project, we can be reasonably sure that it is intended to reflect the present-day student's impulse to learn about life by engaging in honest dialogue with his local and world environment. To the extent that this healthy impulse can find expression, student unrest—along with the other staggering problems of our technological society—will be gradually reduced to a level with which we all can live.

It goes without saying that colleges and universities bold enough to enter uncharted educational waters must be willing to assume the kind of risk which always comes with high adventure. There will be many failures, some of truly awesome proportions. But in time, those new approaches which are found to be effective in one institution will be replicated in others.

The process will never be complete. In what psychologist Warren Bennis has called the "temporary society" of the future, our educational needs will continue to change along with the changing environment. Never again will we be able to afford the luxury of institutions—educational or otherwise—which have no built-in mechanism for transforming themselves in response to evolving human needs. However unpleasant impermanence may be, we shall all have to learn to live with it. We must change, as it were, for change's sake.

The University in Disarray: Causes of Conflict and Prospects for Change*

DAVID P. GARDNER

University of California at Santa Barbara
Santa Barbara, California

"Universities in America are at a hinge of history: while connected with their past they are swinging in another direction."[1] Clark Kerr's apt commentary of six years ago, however sufficient then, no longer adequately describes the revolutionary manifestations for change in the structure and purpose of higher education. The American university faces today not merely a swing "in another direction" but an unhinging from its past. It is a community in disarray with constituents and suitors unrelentingly competing for its invisible and elusive product—the power of organized knowledge.

The causes of conflict in academe, while importantly related to the social malaise currently afflicting the larger community, are primarily to be discovered historically and contemporaneously in its system of governance and balance of interests. The critical variables include (1) the distribution of authority within the university, (2) the order of university priorities, (3) the relationship between academic freedom and university purposes, (4) the changing values of students,

---

*A portion of this paper appeared in the Educational Record, published by the American Council on Education, Spring 1969, pp. 113-120.

13

(5) the reward system, and (6) the curriculum. This paper is an attempt to analyze these variables, calculate their implications, and assess the prospects for change.

Evolution of University Government

The modern American university emerged in the latter half of the nineteenth century with the rise of science and in response to the imperatives of agricultural and industrial expansion. The dominant centers of political and economic power in America early exhibited a vital and expansive interest in the fledgling universities, rewarding men of means and influence with commanding positions in university goverance. But in the twentieth century, the pattern of university government evolved into one that more widely shared responsibility for university affairs and carefully distributed the levers of institutional influence and control. The changes especially favored the faculty, whose authority over educational policy, admissions, faculty appointments, and internal organization increased dramatically.

The road leading to the present structure was long and hard. It was, nevertheless, as willingly traveled by the governing agencies as by the faculty. To put it more directly, it was a *quid pro quo:* in return for the goods, the governing boards gave essential control over the educational process to the faculty. The "goods" were clearly relevant contributions to man's understanding of his natural environment, his institutions, his government, his enemies, and himself. So long as the scholar's pen and the scientist's laboratory yielded such useful knowledge—especially when related to the interests of agriculture, industry, and national security—faculty expectations for meaningful self-government and academic freedom were accommodated.

University priorities in recent decades, therefore, have been dominated by the needs of the advanced industrial state, an enormously profitable arrangement for the nation's productive apparatus on the one hand and for the faculty's well being on the other. Hence, the pattern enjoys the derived stability of a mutually useful alliance. The arrangement, however, is especially discordant at present, for the social, political, and economic goals of vast numbers of students are largely unlike those animating the broader community. Student pressure for change in university process and purpose, therefore, is as understandable as it is predictably resisted, from without by the dominant forces in society and from within by the faculty whose interests continue to be served by the system. The continuing viability of the present pattern, of course, depends in the end on the willingness of the student to acquiesce in a situation made possible primarily by the university's relative neglect of what he perceives as critical to the survival of our society. He is obviously less willing to acquiesce today than before. That is, he is less willing to permit the university's attention, energy, and resources to be expended in the service of external interests regarded by a sizeable proportion of today's student body as less deserving than other more critical and pressing social and environmental problems. In other words, the students are not buying the status quo any more than they are paying for it and their revolt promises inquietude in the nation's institutions of higher learning for the foreseeable future.

Power vs. Principle

The rise of the academician, his dominance over the curriculum and learning experience, his influence over faculty appointments and student admissions, his control of the degree, and his power over the professional organizations have all been essential to the achievement of intellectual maturity in the United States and to the freedom of the scholar to teach, inquire, and publish. But it seems, if current student restiveness is any indicator, that the freedom of the scholar and his control over the learning environment have been nurtured more to advantage the teacher than to impart meaning and relevance to the learner. While it is gladly granted, as Sidney

Hook argues, that "where teachers have no freedom to teach, students have obviously no freedom to learn . . . , " it does not follow that what students wish to learn, teachers choose to teach.[3] And the evidence is everywhere at hand that the disparity is very great, the principal cause being that the curriculum reflects and the teachers teach matter more responsive to the imperatives of professionalism in the academy and to the commands of the surrounding society than to the variegated needs of a highly democratized student body, that is, a student body whose intellectual dispositions, motivations, goals, and cultures are significantly diverse.

The learning process has come to be defined within the context of institutional values as imparted by the faculty on the one hand and by the advanced industrial state on the other. Students whose values are out of harmony with those of their teachers and the larger community—the militant black students, for example—perceive academic freedom, at best, as wholly unrelated to their freedom to learn and, at worst, as the very cause of the university's unresponsiveness to their special needs. Some students respond to the perceived insufficiency of the modern university by founding their own Free Universities. (These places, of course, are as biased as those replaced, for selected values are reflected in each model.) Others seek to enlarge the students' role in the university in order to influence the order of its commitments. Still others, by attacking the reins of administered power in the larger society, attempt to weaken the hold of established influence on university loyalties and ally the incalculable power of organized knowledge with new causes—for example, away from agriculture and toward urban problems, away from armaments and toward poverty in America.

Students argue increasingly that the university can no longer stand disinterestedly in the midst of social turmoil, or claim neutrality as a reason for noninvolvement in the social ills of the day. But even if the university refuses to intervene, it is asserted, then at least it should not be permitted to prevent its students from doing so. This conflict over student involvement in social and political causes *qua* student, which many argue on educational, not on political or civil grounds, has already radically modified the scope of university authority over student activism.

Those who oppose students implicating the university in social and political issues have argued the inevitability of the surrounding society answering in kind, thus threatening the institutions supposed autonomy. In response, it has been asserted that the university is already enmeshed in the military and industrial imperatives of the larger society, and to suppose it free of political influence evades reality; massive university ties to the Atomic Energy Commission, the Department of Defense, and the agricultural lobby are examples.

The university cannot, the dissidents argue, work both sides of the street. It cannot, for example, opt to engage its resources in behalf of the Institute for Defense Analyses, pleading service to the state, and be disinterested in the civil rights movement, alleging institutional neutrality. The argument is double-edged, of course, for it can be made in reverse. Thus, the character of much of the conflict in higher education is illuminated. It is a power struggle to convert the university from one set of concerns to another, for example, from weapons research to the elimination of poverty, from the development of tomato harvesters to the educational problems of migrant children, from a concern with pesticides to the social problems of the inner city; in short, from objects to more direct and immediate human needs.

Politicized University

It is not simply a matter, however, of rearranging priorities. It is one also of making distinctions between political inquiry, expression, learning, and teaching, and the use of the university primarily to stage and execute political demonstrations, organize and manage political campaigns, and plan and direct social movements. If one cannot make meaningful distinctions here, then one might as well count the university as a third political party, an institution as politicized as it would be anti-intellectual, with an ethos favoring coercion over persuasion, intimidation over reason, threat over thought, and duress over dialogue. The description may already fit, at least to whatever extent confrontation politics increasingly dictates the resolution of differences within the academy.

If the university were to advocate the political refashioning of the larger society along particular lines it would become merely another instrument of social revolution bent on weaving the political, social, and economic fabric of our culture into a different pattern. Such a politically partisan commitment would necessarily bind the university's constituent elements and fundamentally alter its structure and purpose. And it cannot be pleaded that the description already fits. While it is one thing for the centers of power in our society to dictate the balance of interests in the university and to apply the abundant yield in ways that serve the productive apparatus of the technologically advanced state, it is quite another for the individual scholar and scientist to be bound by the institution to partisan causes. The difference is the viability of individual intellectual freedom, the very touchstone of a true university. For example, while federal contracts and grants for research in public health, agriculture, weaponry, and space have in substantial measure ordered university priorities by claiming a disproportionate share of its material and human resources, this fact does not bind the scientist intellectually in his work on these problems, any more than a foundation funding a study of migrant workers binds the social scientist to other than his own conclusions. The influencing of university priorities and concerns is not at all the same thing as the politically partisan commitment that admits to a surrender of intellectual freedom, for the options are inclusive in the commitment. Thus, one cannot hope corporately to commit the university to partisanship of a political sort without also binding its parts, any more than one can expect coercion as a style to exist side by side with persuasion in an institution dependent more on reason than on passion for its work.

The argument is not meant, however, to refute or doubt the legitimacy of calls for a realigning of interests in the university or the legitimacy of partisanship by individual members of the faculty or student body acting as private citizens in a free society. But, a reordering of university interests to accommodate social problems at the upper levels of university consciousness by making them objects of educational purpose promises to be more disruptive of university-community relationships than when such expressions of concern were less favored than the production of value-neutral technology. This will be especially true if faculty members blur the distinctions between their rights as citizens and their responsibilities as scholars, the first denying the teacher special treatment in the broader society, and the second preserving for the teacher a special position and protection in the university.[4]

But the student, who is most often neither franchised in the larger society nor credentialed in the academy, has no distinctions to blur except for those responsibilities imposed on him by the university and those rights securing his constitutionally protected liberties. It should not be surprising, therefore, that he has chosen to exercise his civilly assured rights to rid himself of institutionally obtruded constraints and thus to invite an analogy between the university and the civil community, one that pressures the university to adopt civilly accepted rather than academically derived concepts of structure, process, and style.[5]

The turmoil in American higher education today results not so much from efforts to destroy the university as from the competition of its suitors, whose dissimilar social, political, and economic goals impinge directly on the rights and responsibilities of members of the university community, that is, on the freedoms that have traditionally been associated with the structure and process of our institutions of higher learning. For example, students have recently won the freedom at a number of universities to organize on campus for off-campus political action, to recruit volunteers and solicit funds on campus for off-campus social causes, to make university facili-

ties available to off-campus speakers whose remarks are not
subject to prior review by university authorities: in short, to
engage university facilities and members in a super abundance
of political and social activity. The rather vigorous use of these
freedoms by students has already influenced university inten-
tions which in turn have implicated the authority pattern and
the decision-making processes within the university. Thus, as
the objects of university concern shift away from a preoccupation with logical positivism and the production of technology
and toward a commitment to more encompassing values and
principles, there will also very likely occur a simultaneous
restructuring of the university's authority system to include
representative elements of the student body in institutional
centers of power. In any event, new compacts must be conceived in the university among those whose rights and responsibilities are interrelated, and whose interests compete or conflict. While much is negotiable in constructing new treaties,
intellectual freedom is not. There can be no accommodation
with those whose political commitments are more important
than the intellectual freedom of others, a principle increasingly
compromised by the more aggressive elements of the student
community who seemingly little regard either the academic
freedoms or those protected by civil law. The prospect of losing
these freedoms is not to be dismissed lightly, given the mili-
tancy of that element and the timidity with which recent viola-
tions of others' rights have been condemned by the academic
community.

Professionalism and Teaching in the University

To realign university priorities and structure in ways more
consistent with student expectations and goals than with the
immediate requirements of the technologically advanced state
responds only partially, however, to the overall problem of
bringing into harmony the educational norms, standards, and
expectations of the faculty on the one hand, and the needs,
desires, and hopes of an increasingly differentiated undergradu-

ate student body on the other. Students differ from each other in style, identity, orientation, commitment, complexity, autonomy, and values quite as much as they do in interest and ability. And so, obviously, do faculty members differ from one another in similar ways. But as Joseph Katz and his associates have made abundantly clear in *No Time For Youth*, colleges have not sufficiently linked these varied styles and approaches to their educational tasks.[6] Instead, higher education in the United States has preferred to measure and standardize educational progress and achievement by quantifying course and classroom experience, as Bradford Cleaveland harshly observed of the Berkeley model just prior to the "Free Speech Movement" that so disrupted that campus in 1964:

> The salient characteristic of the multiversity is massive production of specialized excellence. The multiversity is actually not an educational center but a highly efficient industry engaged in producing skilled individuals to meet the immediate needs of business and government . . .

> Below the level of formal power and responsibility (the Regents, president and chancellors), the faculty itself is guilty of a massive and disastrous default. More concerned with their own increasingly affluent specialized careers, they have permitted an administrative process to displace, and become an obstruction to, extended thought and learning for the undergraduate . . .

> The process [of education] is a four-year-long series of sharp staccatos: eight semesters, forty courses, one hundred twenty or more "units," ten to fifteen impersonal lectures *per week*, and one to three oversized discussion meetings per week led by poorly paid, unlearned graduate students.[7]

Cleaveland's hostility centered on the faculty for what he perceived to be their collective neglect of the undergraduate in favor of their own collective aggrandizement. Undergraduate education, those of Cleaveland's persuasion argued, had been usurped and demeaned in favor of a bureaucracy fashioned as much by the faculty as by the administration. The system thus contrived favored precision, efficiency, speed, control, continuity, and similar measures which optimized returns on input, depersonalized human relationships, and minimized nonrational considerations. In short, the faculty, by their preoccupation with research, consulting, and graduate instruction had given the goals of undergraduate education over to these bureaucratic processes.

The diminished role of teaching in the university, of which the educational dysfunctions noted above are symptomatic, are attributable primarily (1) to a reward system that favors production of knowledge over the cultivation of young minds, (2) to a scarcity of able men in relation to demand whose resulting opportunities permit them to dictate terms of employment that assure high visibility (i.e., a distribution of time that favors research and writing over teaching), and (3) to a shift of faculty loyalties from the university to the academic profession and the research granting agencies. While these realities do not require the individual faculty member to opt for research over teaching, they do indicate the cost individual members of the profession must be prepared to pay if they choose the reverse emphasis. To favor teaching over research within the present context is to discount the prospective value of the faculty member's worth measured on any scale other than his own personal satisfaction and whatever derived benefit his students enjoy because of his greater interest in them than in his own professional advancement.

Teaching and research are not, of course, as exclusive as they have thus far been made out to be. Indeed, they are complementary at the level of graduate instruction and to a lesser extent at the undergraduate level. But the reward system, a seller's market, and a waning of institutional loyalty allows the faculty member, if he chooses, to push student needs down the scale of university priorities while moving his own to the top. *To put it bluntly, the production of knowledge not the education of the student is the overriding preoccupation of the modern American university.* Were the great bulk of students as professionally oriented as their teachers, the grave dysfunctions of the present arrangement would be greatly moderated. But they are not, and the ever increasing diversity of the American university undergraduate student body promises to create more not less discontent among a growing proportion of students, especially among those studying the social sciences and humanities.

Changing Values

When societal expectations and those of the great majority of students were in harmony, as was generally true when the veterans of World War II inundated America's colleges and universities in the late 1940s and early 1950s, the educational experience was minimally dysfunctional, however uneven the quality of instruction may have been and however crowded were the conditions. But if the educational expectations of students change and those of the larger society do not (a fair but highly generalized observation of the contemporary educational scene), then educational dysfunction is predictable.

The values that shaped the present condition of modern man in America are chiefly those embodied in the Protestant ethic of hard work and achievement in a highly competitive social milieu. "Thrift, self-discipline, hard work, asceticism, worldliness—these and similar characteristics of the Protestant ethic," Max Weber has observed, "nurtured the conditions necessary for the development of capitalism, modern science, and bureaucratic organization—all of which support one another to a large degree."[8] But the Protestant ethic, William H. Whyte, Jr. has argued, no longer meaningfully functions in American life, it having been replaced by a bureaucracy which has become the controlling end in itself.[9] Thus, modern man looks less to the ethic for meaning and security in society than to the big organization—corporation, government, military, church, labor union, and professional association. On his ability to move effectively among these organized units, hinges not only the individual's claim to income, success, and security, but the viability, rationality, and efficiency of the organizational system itself. Thus, the attributes of organization man are carefully nurtured by society, the essential ones being (1) a desire to achieve, (2) an ability to postpone gratification, (3) a tolerance for frustration, (4) a willingness to compromise, and (5) a capacity and drive for disciplined work. These qualities reflect organizational imperatives for commitment, career aspirations, functional expertise, rational behavior, and cooperation.

Whether Whyte's observations about the submergence of the Protestant ethic to the organizational needs of the society it created are generally valid or not, it is surely true that the values of the ethic are waning in importance as the scientific and cybernetic revolution supplant the earlier industrial revolution. And it is the newer revolution not the older one that the younger generation will live through; and the university student senses that his education inadequately anticipates the changes in values, life styles, and patterns of work with which he will be confronted. Instead, his education largely reflects the priorities, expectations, and personality preferences of the earlier generation whose own sense of identity, individual worth, and security are interwoven with the older values that formed contemporary society. Thus, for the student to reject the older values and the society it produced is to threaten not only the established order but also the viability of an educational process designed not to modify or alter the system but to nurture and sustain it. But for the student to accept those same values and the institutions that dictate the conditions of life in contemporary society is to compromise his own perception of the world in which he will live the greater part of his mature years. And in a rapidly changing world, the student is impatient with and insensitive to a university more committed to serving the established order than to preparing the student for the social, cultural, religious, political, and environmental dislocations with which his generation will be expected to cope.

The Learning Process

The American university, as Max Lerner puts it, "is the

convergence point of the major revolutionary forces of our time."[10] And it is largely a values revolution, one, therefore, that insists upon an examination of the contemporary scene within the totality of the culture. The university curriculum, therefore, is relevant for the student to whatever extent it seeks systematically to communicate the vital ideas of the culture, to establish relationships, to tie historical evidence to discernible trends, and to synthesize knowledge into a cohesive whole where the parts are understood in relationship to each other as critically as they are perceived separately. But the undergraduate curriculum in American higher education has evolved more in response to the research interests of the faculty than to the learning requirements of the student. Instead of breadth in the curriculum, there is mostly proliferation. In place of unity, there is unrelatedness. Rather than synthesis and cohesion, there is atomization. Moreover, the stress is on educating students to man the productive components of the industrial complex rather than on educating them to live with and participate in the problems and derived benefits of the scientific and cybernetic society.

The teaching and research interest and experience of the faculty determine the character and content of the curriculum, and these traditionally center on what Katz calls the "academic-conceptual area" with an emphasis on subject matter, analysis, description, hypothesis, and cognitive rationality. The curriculum thus devised is essentially devoid of what could be a more encompassing and larger learning environment. In other words, the faculty, and therefore the curriculum, dwell nearly exclusively on but one of several discernible teaching and learning areas, thus favoring students disposed toward the academic-conceptual model and disadvantaging students for whom reality and learning are best understood and carried on within different contexts, e.g., those stressing esthetics, emotions, feelings, and sensibilities; those preferring the affective domain; those responding to people-oriented activities and services; those favoring inanimate or artificial objects; those preferring motoric expression; those wishing for the development of skills in human relations, social ability, friendship, and intimacy in the human experience.

Because the faculty perceives its teaching responsibilities primarily within the academic-conceptual model, the measures and standards that determine access to and exit from higher education are understandably reflections of that bias. Thus, grade point average in a core curriculum, units completed, and numbers of courses taken in subject-matter fields standardize and quantify students in ways that systematically push out all but the one teaching and learning area that presently predominates. To make room for the others would require major changes in criteria and curricular offerings. These would be as insistent and demanding as the present, but differentiated to accommodate differences in student characteristics that bear on achievement and performance.

If such changes were to be made, they would necessarily emphasize a complete program for the development of the individual student in contrast to the existing disconnected, fragmented, and partial approach that is so clearly a reflection of the knowledge rather than the student-oriented university. But such programs would compromise the essential dominance of the academic departments over the curriculum, whose structures of disciplines and courses, as Nevitt Sanford has observed, "were designed less for the purpose of teaching than for the production of knowledge."[11] And the issue is thus joined. On the one hand, the career aspirations of the faculty are currently so interwoven with the integrity and power of the academic department that any proposal to modify the effective control of the department over the reward system and the curriculum would be met with the faculty's tenacious and unrelenting resistence. On the other hand, the educational aspirations of an increasing number of students are inconsistent with the fragmented curriculum and the professional bias of the faculty whose pursuit of specialized knowledge continues to be more highly regarded and rewarded than is their work with students. An accommodation of these critical differences may very well be preceded by an intense and prolonged confrontation between the students and the faculty.

The members of the faculty, of course, are in an uncomfortable position. On the one hand, they rely on the stability of their existing interface with the dominant interests in society for the resources necessary to undertake research, and on the other hand, they depend on the willingness of the students to cooperate in an arrangement made possible primarily by the university's neglect of them. The reward system as presently operative supports the viability and congruence of the faculty's research interests and the prevailing requirements of the technologically advanced state, as already noted. But the current escalation of student discontent suggests that higher education is at the point of having to grapple with the malfunctions of the system if the university's essential character is to survive. This will mean not only a reordering of priorities and the involvement of students in the authority system as noted in the early part of this paper, but it will also require major modifications of the educational experience including the criteria used to admit and graduate students. And finally, it will mean that the educational environment must necessarily be as diverse in approach, methodology, and outcome as the student body it chooses to serve is varied in style, motivation, values, and expectation.

The changes in university priorities, structure, and curriculum can be made only if the faculty chooses to make them and indirectly if the society wishes to pay for them. Whether basic modifications will be made voluntarily or only after persistent and extended student discontent will largely determine if higher education in the United States preserves or loses the freedom and self-determination that are regarded as essential to the integrity of its mission and the individual intellectual freedom of those dedicated to its noble principles.

28 DAVID P. GARDNER

REFERENCES AND NOTES

1. Clark Kerr, *The Uses of the University* (Cambridge: Harvard University Press, 1963), p. 2.
2. Charles Frankel, *Education and the Barricades* (New York: W. W. Norton and Co., 1968). Consult this work for a contrary view that ascribes student unrest primarily to problems beyond the campus.
3. Sidney Hook, "Democracy Doesn't Work on Campus," *Los Angeles Times*, 19 May 1968.
4. Richard F. Schier, "Academic Freedom and Political Action," *AAUP Bulletin*, Spring 1967, pp. 22–26. Consult this article for a fuller discussion of this point.
5. Martin Trow, "Conceptions of the University," *American Behavioral Scientist*, May–June 1968, especially p. 19. Consult this article for a fuller discussion of this point.
6. Joseph Katz et al., *No Time for Youth* (San Francisco: Jossey-Bass, 1968), p. 421.
7. Bradford Cleaveland, "Education, Revolutions, and Citadels," *The Berkeley Student Revolt*, ed. S. M. Lipset and S. S. Wolin (New York: Anchor Books, 1965), pp. 89–90.
8. Max Weber, *The Protestant Ethic and the Spirit of Capitalism*, trans. Talcott Parsons (New York: Charles Scribner's Sons, 1958).
9. William H. Whyte, Jr., *The Organization Man* (Garden City, N. Y.: Anchor Books, 1957).
10. Max Lerner, "The Revolutionary Frame of Our Time," *The College and the Student*, ed. Lawrence Dennis and Joseph Kaufman (Washington, D.C.: American Council on Education, 1966), p. 8.
11. Nevitt Sanford, *Where Colleges Fail* (San Francisco: Jossey-Bass, 1967), p. xiv.

Comparative Statistics on Campus Turmoil 1964-1968

RAYMOND TANTER

The University of Michigan
Ann Arbor, Michigan

The following compilation of statistics on campus turmoil was developed to provide a general overview of the situation in the nation's universities from Berkeley to Columbia for the years 1964 to 1968. Further study might yield a more theoretically significant, detailed, and reliable set of data.*

One purpose in collecting these statistics was to evaluate turmoil in terms of its consequences. Much of the literature on conflict seeks to explain it rather than to assess its effect. One of the problems in ascertaining specific effects of turmoil is the fact that it is difficult to measure long term effects.

For example, consider the case of the University of California, Berkeley's Free Speech Movement (FSM) in 1964. The initial goal of FSM was to protest the restriction of political activity on the campus, such as not allowing booths to provide information about various organizations. Escalation of the protest brought new issues into the dispute such as the suspension of students, size of classes, etc. Unintended consequences of

*Acknowledgments and appreciation to the National Science Foundation for support; to Michael Shaul and Judith Tanter for research assistance; to Irving L. Horowitz for the use of certain of his data; and to the American Society for Cybernetics for the opportunity to present these statistics at its Third Annual Conference.

FSM activity are also relevant. For instance, turmoil at Berkeley may have had the unexpected effect of increasing faculty
salaries and decreasing teaching loads. That is, the turmoil
resulted in raids on Berkeley's faculty by other institutions such
as Harvard. These offers to the faculty increased their bargaining position for higher salaries and lighter teaching loads.
This was especially true for some of the more highly-visible
members of the faculty. Clearly, it is exceedingly difficult to
assess the effects of campus turmoil beyond these few immediate and obvious consequences.

Another theoretical purpose in the compilation of these
statistics is to discover the degree to which turmoil is becoming less oriented toward programmatic goals in favor of disruption for the sake of disruption. Again, it is difficult to assess
whether the struggle is to achieve concrete goals or if, as has
been suggested by I. L. Horowitz, the struggle itself is the
message.[1]

Theoretical interest in whether or not campus struggle itself
was becoming the message derives from observing the contrast between the strategies of black militants and white radicals in the events in April and May 1968 at Columbia University. The initial issues were Columbia's intention to construct a gymnasium in Morningside Heights and its involvement with the Institute for Defense Analyses. As in the Berkeley FSM situation, Columbia protests escalated, providing opportunities for presenting new demands.

Black militants appeared to take advantage of the situation
in a more rational manner than did white radicals. Black students' demands were worked out more adequately and they
discussed objectives on which the administration could deliver,
whereas some of the white students followed a strategy of
disruption for the sake of disruption. Also, they followed a
policy of "theatrical protest." The theater of politics fit in very
nicely with the comic antics of Yippie leader Abbie Hoffman.
Theoretical interest in whether there is indeed an increase in
the theatrical quality of protests was difficult to translate into
empirical coding. Hence, there is little reference to this in the
statistics that follow.

Another theoretical interest that helped to guide the compilation of statistics on the subject of campus turmoil concerns ideas about escalation. Certain authors and administrators contend that the threat of official reprisal should be an effective deterrent to student protest. Calling the police onto campus at an early stage, they assert, would prevent later protest escalation. Others, however, claim that calling the police onto campus early tends to escalate the turmoil by affording the protesting students a new issue around which to mobilize. This deterrence/escalation theme proved as difficult to translate into coding rules as did the earlier theoretical issues being considered here.

In summary, three questions stimulated the data acquisition: 1. What are the effects of turmoil? 2. Is turmoil becoming more theatrical and less rational in nature? 3. What is the role of the police in deterring or escalating turmoil? These questions proved difficult to translate into empirical coding rules, given the available sources for an inquiry. This paper, therefore, presents only speculations, based on the statistics, and not definite conclusions.

Turmoil, it would seem, often produces consequences which protesters have neither intended nor expected. A typical pattern of this may be that original goals are replaced by new purposes consistent with the ensuing struggle. For instance, at Berkeley, when the demand for amnesty replaced the demand for free speech as a goal, one of the unexpected results was the strengthening of judiciary organs within the university. Also, since faculty tends to form a coalition with either the students or the administration, an unintended consequence may turn out to be an increase in the power of the faculty. In several recent instances, the balance of power has tended to reside in whichever side the faculty decided to join.

On the issue of whether turmoil is becoming more theatrical, there is even less to derive from the statistics. Almost all of the 108 incidents contain information on the issues and on the techniques used. In each case a technique appropriate to the issue at hand seems to have been used. There is a problem with this interpretation, however. It assumes that there is a homogeneous group of students that pickets, boycotts, strikes, or riots. The Yippie-like element, however, tends to surface during an on-going conventional student protest. It is difficult to separate the activities of the clowns from those of the more political elements. The speculation is that there is an increase in the more comic activity, but the absolute level of such antics is still very small in the overall picture.

At the University of Michigan, for example, activist students separate into several groups. One split is between the Radical Caucus and the Jesse James Gang. Radical Caucus is a fairly large issue oriented coalition, while the Jesse James Gang is a small hippie-type group, largely without issues. A speech by President Robben Fleming provided an illustration of the hippie technique. The Jesse James Gang passed out bread to persons entering the auditorium, stating that they would receive the balony inside from the President!

With regard to the deterrence/escalation issue, the early use of police appears not to deter so much as to provoke a larger coalition to form against the administration. Once violence occurs, however, the presence of large numbers of police or national guardsmen appears to be effective in deterring further violence. One of the interesting points related to the deterrence question is the small number of police involvements (twelve) compared to the number of total incidents (108). That is, based on the data presented here, police came on campus in about ten percent of the incidents. The ten percent figure, however, does not say anything about the timing of police moves. From a spot check of the chronologies reported in the news sources, though, it seems as if the presence of police on campus *before* violence occurred actually provoked violence. However, the absence of police on campus, once violence had begun, prolonged and/or increased the violence.

In conclusion, three theoretical issues stimulated this acquisition of information on campus turmoil. Unfortunately, the information is only indirectly relevant to answering these issues.

The following tables contain data on 108 incidents from May 1964 to August 1968. The 108 incidents recorded spread unevenly across some fifty universities, involving between 100,000 and 300,000 persons. As regards the number of incidents per school, the following is a ranking of campuses from high to low: Columbia, Berkeley, CCNY, Wisconsin, Cornell, and Chicago.

The procedure for collecting the data slightly biases the data in favor of anti-war protests over other issues. Some of the information was based on an appendix to a paper by Irving L. Horowitz, *The Struggle Is the Message*, 1968, prepared for The National Commission on the Causes and Prevention of Violence; the September 1969 issue of *Esquire*, which contained a list of additional campuses suffering turmoil; *The New York Times* Index from January 1, 1964 to August 31, 1968; and *The New York Times* Microfilm file. *No reliability tests were performed on the coding. The author does not guarantee the reliability of the figures.* They are meant to be suggestive of what happened rather than to be definitive. The abbreviations used in the tables are:

BAS	Black Student Alliance
SAS	Society of Afro-American Students
SFCAR	Student-Faculty Coalition Against Racism
FSM	Free Speech Movement
NCC	National Coordinating Committee to End the War in Vietnam
SGC	Student Government Council
IDA	Institute for Defense Analyses
NYT	*The New York Times*
ILH	Irving L. Horowitz
ESQ	*Esquire* Magazine
UMOISA	The name, not an abbreviation, of Boston University's Black Student organization.

REFERENCES

1. *The Struggle Is the Message*, a paper by Irving L. Horowitz, 1968, prepared for the National Commission on the Causes and Prevention of Violence.

A COMPARATIVE ANALYSIS OF CAMPUS TURMOIL

Date	University	National Issue	Local Issue	Technique	Duration (in days)	No. of Students	Position of Faculty
5/22/64	C.C.N.Y.	speech by Ross Barnett		eggs thrown and heckling	1	2,000	favor issue
6/11/64	U.C.L.A.		protest honorary degree to Shah of Iran	picket, walk out	1	4	
9/30/64 10/ 2/64	U.C.B. (Berkeley)		restriction of political activity by UCB(FSM)	rally, hold police captive, sit-in	3	300	
11/10/64	U.C.B.		F.S.M.	petition	1	100 grad & T.F.	T.F. support
12/ 2/64	U.C.B.		F.S.M.	take over Ad Bldg.	1	2,000	divided support
12/ 3/64	U.C.B.		F.S.M.	rally	1	5,000	
12/ 4/64	U.C.B.		F.S.M.	picket, strike	1	10,000	
12/ 7/64	U.C.B.		F.S.M.	rally	1	13,000	
12/ 8/64	Harvard, Radcliffe, Brandeis, Tufts & Simmons		support for F.S.M. at U.C.B.	march and rally	1	200 student faculty	
3/ 1/65	Yale		anti-publish or perish	picket	1	50	support
3/26/65	Brooklyn College		anti-loyalty oath	rally	1	500	support
3/29/65	Brooklyn College		lack of academic freedom	walk-out	1	200	some support
4/21/65	Columbia		tuition increase	petition	1	300	
4/22/65	U.C.B.		suspension of four students	rally	1	1,500	
4/23/65	Ohio State		controversial speaker ban	sit-in	1	250	
4/24/65	Duke	KKK heckled Vice-Pres. Humphrey		heckle KKK	1	over 300	

A COMPARATIVE ANALYSIS OF CAMPUS TURMOIL (Cont'd)

Date	Reaction of Administration	No. of Students Arrested	Injuries to Students	Injuries to Authorities	On/Off Campus Police	Property Damage	Organizers	Long Term Effect	Sources
5/22/64									N.Y.T.
6/11/64									N.Y.T.
9/30/64 10/ 2/64									N.Y.T.
11/10/64	threaten suspension						FSM		N.Y.T.
12/ 2/64	Gov. Brown orders removal after 12 hrs.	641 (& 163 non-students)			off		FSM		N.Y.T.
12/ 3/64							FSM		N.Y.T.
12/ 4/64							FSM		N.Y.T.
12/ 7/64	police harass speaker	none			on		FSM		N.Y.T.
12/ 8/64									N.Y.T.
3/ 1/65									N.Y.T.
3/26/65									N.Y.T.
3/29/65									N.Y.T.
4/21/65									N.Y.T.
4/22/65									N.Y.T.
4/23/65	agree to review ban							trustees vote 5-3 to keep ban (7/65)	N.Y.T.
4/24/65									N.Y.T.

A COMPARATIVE ANALYSIS OF CAMPUS TURMOIL (Cont'd)

Date	University	National Issue	Local Issue	Technique	Duration (in days)	No. of Students	Position of Faculty
5/ 7/65	Columbia	Vietnam		rally	1	200	
7/29/65	U.C.B.		sentence for Dec.1964 sit-ins too harsh	rally, march	1	1,000 500	
10/15/65	Boston U.	Vietnam		rally	1	750	
10/15/65	Wayne State	Vietnam		teach-in	1	400	
10/15/65	Santa Barbara	Vietnam		rally	1	300	
10/15/65	Colorado	Vietnam		rally	1	100	
10/15/65	Iowa State	Vietnam		picket USNR	1	12	
10/15/65	Yale	Vietnam		rally	1	250	
10/15/65	C.C.N.Y.	Vietnam		rally and vigil	1	600	
10/16/65	Penn	Vietnam		march	1	350	
10/16/65	Cornell	Vietnam		silent vigil	1	300	
10/28/65	Washington U.	speech by HHH		picket	1	40	
12/ 4/65	Fordham		banishment of Berrigan	rally	1	50	
2/ 3/66	Brynmawr, Swarthmore, Haverford	Vietnam		fast	8	175	
5/12/66	U. of Chicago	draft ranking		sit-in	1	350	
5/13/66	C.C.N.Y.	draft		sit-in	1	150	
5/18/66	Wisconsin	draft	support Ad Bldg. take-over		1	10,000	
5/19/66	Brooklyn	draft		sit-in	1	75	

A COMPARATIVE ANALYSIS OF CAMPUS TURMOIL (Cont'd)

Date	Reaction of Administration	No. of Students Arrested	Injuries to Students	Injuries to Authorities	On/Off Campus Police	Property Damage	Organizers	Long Term Effect	Sources
5/ 7/65									I.L.H.
7/29/65									N.Y.T.
10/15/65									I.L.H.
10/15/65									I.L.H.
10/15/65									I.L.H.
10/15/65									I.L.H.
10/15/65									I.L.H.
10/15/65									I.L.H.
10/15/65									I.L.H.
10/16/65							NCC		I.L.H.
10/16/65									I.L.H.
10/28/65							SDS		I.L.H.
12/ 4/65									I.L.H.
2/ 3/66									I.L.H.
5/12/66							SDS & NCC		I.L.H.
5/13/66									I.L.H.
5/18/66									I.L.H.
5/19/66									I.L.H.

A COMPARATIVE ANALYSIS OF CAMPUS TURMOIL (Cont'd)

Date	University	National Issue	Local Issue	Technique	Duration (in days)	No. of Students	Position of Faculty
5/19/66	Roosevelt U.	draft		sit-in	1		
5/24/66	Hunter	draft		demonstrations	1		
6/ 3/66	Amherst	honorary degree to R. S. McNamara		walk-out	1	20	
8/ 6/66	Wisconsin	ROTC		vigil	1	(approx.)10	
11/ 7/66	Harvard	McNamara speech		shout him down, lie under car	1	100 25	
11/15/66	Brown	Gen.Wheeler speech		rally	1	100	
11/15/66	Columbia	CIA recruiting		blocked doorway	1	100	
11/21/66	Columbia	CIA recruiting		rally	1	500	
11/29/66	Michigan		student voice in U decisions	sit-in	1	1,500	
12/ 1/66	U.C.B.	military recruitment		boycott classes	6	5,000	opposed
12/ 2/66	Columbia		show support for U.C.B.	rally	1	150	
12/ 6/66	N.Y.U.		tuition increase	rally, sit-in	1	800	
12/ 8/66	N.Y.U.		tuition increase	strike, picket, sit-in	1	5,000, 200 350	
12/ 8/66	C.C.N.Y.	Army recruiters		sit-in	1	34	
1/20/67	Cornell		censorship of campus magazine	riot	1	1,000	
1/22/67	Wisconsin	Dow recruiter			1	100	
2/ 8/67	Columbia	CIA recruiting		sit-in	1	19	

A COMPARATIVE ANALYSIS OF CAMPUS TURMOIL (Cont'd)

Date	Reaction of Administration	No. of Students Arrested	Injuries to Students	Injuries to Authorities	On/Off Campus Police	Property Damage	Organizers	Long Term Effect	Sources
5/19/66									I.L.H.
5/24/66									I.L.H.
6/ 3/66									N.Y.T.
8/ 6/66									I.L.H.
11/ 7/66	police called	1			off		SDS		I.L.H., N.Y.T.
11/15/66									I.L.H.
11/15/66							SDS		N.Y.T.
11/21/66							SDS		N.Y.T.
11/29/66							SGC		N.Y.T.
12/ 1/66									N.Y.T.
12/ 2/66									N.Y.T.
12/ 6/66	delay R & B raise, keep tuition increase								N.Y.T.
12/ 8/66									N.Y.T.
12/ 8/66	students suspended for 8 days								N.Y.T.
1/20/67	attempt to arrest sellers of magazine				off				N.Y.T.
1/22/67		18					SDS		I.L.H.
2/ 8/67	call off interviews								N.Y.T.

A COMPARATIVE ANALYSIS OF CAMPUS TURMOIL (Cont'd)

Date	University	National Issue	Local Issue	Technique	Duration (in days)	No. of Students	Position of Faculty
2/13/67	Harvard	A. Goldberg speech		march	1	500	
2/20/67	Columbia		hearing on 19 who sat-in Feb. 8	disrupt hearing	1	100	
3/30/67	C.C.N.Y.		plan to limit Business School to jrs., srs., and grads	picket	1	1,000	
4/11/67	Wisconsin	CIA recruiting		demonstrate	1	500	
5/11/67	Radcliffe		restrictions on apartment living	fast	1	19	
5/17/67	U.C.L.A.	anti-Rhodesia		rally	1	200	
10/ 8/67	Williams	Lady Bird speech		walkout	1	75	
10/ 9/67	Yale	Lady Bird speech		silent vigil	1	750	
10/18/67	Wisconsin	anti-Dow		riot	1	1,000	
10/19/67	Brooklyn	Navy recruitment		sit-in	1	1,000	support
10/20/67	Brooklyn		police brutality of Oct. 19	strike	1	8,000	support
10/20/67	Columbia	CIA recruiting and IDA support		demonstrate	1	300	
10/23/67	Princeton	IDA support		sit-in	1	50	
10/24/67	Minnesota	Dow		sleep-in Ad Bldg.	1	20	
10/25/67	Illinois	Dow		picket	1	300	
10/25/67	Harvard	Dow		sit-in, hold recruiter prisoner	1	200	

A COMPARATIVE ANALYSIS OF CAMPUS TURMOIL (Cont'd)

Date	Reaction of Administration	No. of Students Arrested	Injuries to Students	Injuries to Authorities	On/Off Campus Police	Property Damage	Organizers	Long Term Effect	Sources
2/13/67							SDS		I.L.H.
2/20/67									N.Y.T.
3/30/67									N.Y.T.
4/11/67									N.Y.T.
5/11/67									N.Y.T.
5/17/67			9						N.Y.T.
10/ 8/67									NYT,ILH
10/ 9/67									I.L.H.
10/18/67			70			some buildings			I.L.H.
10/19/67	200 police called in	40 students & faculty			off				I.L.H.
10/20/67									I.L.H.
10/20/67							SDS		I.L.H.
10/23/67							SDS		I.L.H.
10/24/67									I.L.H.
10/25/67									I.L.H.
10/25/67									I.L.H.

A COMPARATIVE ANALYSIS OF CAMPUS TURMOIL (Cont'd)

Date	University	National Issue	Local Issue	Technique	Duration (in days)	No. of Students	Position of Faculty
10/26/67	Oberlin	Navy recruitment		surround car		100	
11/ 1/67	C.C.N.Y.		construction of pre-fab classroom bldg.	obstructing work	1	49	
11/ 1/67	U. of Iowa	Marine recruiting		sit-in	1	108	
11/ 1/67	Penn.	CIA & Dow recruiting		sit-in	1	150	
11/ 1/67	Stanford	CIA & Dow recruiting		peaceful demonstration	1	120	
11/ 2/67	C.C.N.Y.		Pre-fabs	strike	2	500	
11/ 6/67	Chicago	Dow		picket	1	500	
11/ 6/67	U.C.B.	CIA & Dow		picket	1	250	
11/11/67	Columbia		Morningside gym	burn trustee's effigy	1	40	
11/17/67	Cornell	Marine recruitment		demonstrate	1	200	
11/20/67	San Jose	Dow		demonstrate	1	2,000	
11/29/67	N.Y.U.	Dow		demonstrate	1	200	
1/24/68	Ohio State	Marine recruitment		sit-in and debate	1	200	
2/ 1/68	Ohio State		discrimination	protest	1	100 black	
2/ 6/68	Maine	Dow		protest	1	300	
2/11/68	Harvard, Radcliffe, Boston U.	Vietnam		fast	4	400	
2/14/68	Amherst	Dow & Chase Bank		burn napalm effigy	1	350	
2/14/68	Washington	Dow		protest	1	60	
2/20/68	Columbia		Morningside gym	obstruct work	1	12	

A COMPARATIVE ANALYSIS OF CAMPUS TURMOIL (Cont'd)

Date	Reaction of Administration	No. of Students Arrested	Injuries to Students	Injuries to Authorities	On/Off Campus Police	Property Damage	Organizers	Long Term Effect	Sources
10/26/67	police use tear gas								I.L.H.
11/ 1/67	first plea, then police	49			off	student government			N.Y.T.
11/ 1/67	used police	108			off				N.Y.T.
11/ 1/67									N.Y.T.
11/ 1/67									N.Y.T.
11/ 2/67		2			off				N.Y.T.
11/ 6/67									N.Y.T.
11/ 6/67									N.Y.T.
11/11/67									N.Y.T.
11/17/67	50 police w/tear gas	some			off				N.Y.T.
11/20/67									I.L.H.
11/29/67									I.L.H.
1/24/68									I.L.H.
2/ 1/68									N.Y.T.
2/ 6/68	police prevent action								I.L.H.
2/11/68									I.L.H.
2/14/68									I.L.H.
2/14/68	postpone interviews						SDS		I.L.H.
2/20/68		12			off				N.Y.T.

A COMPARATIVE ANALYSIS OF CAMPUS TURMOIL (Cont'd)

Date	University	National Issue	Local Issue	Technique	Duration (in days)	No. of Students	Position of Faculty
2/24/68	American U.	HHH speech		walk-out	1	75	
2/27/68	Iona	Dow		protest	1	150	
2/28/68	Columbia		Morningside gym	protest	1	150	
3/12/68	Yale		discrimination	strike	2	72 blacks	
4/ 5/68	Cornell		racist remarks of professor	7 hr.siege of Econ bldg.	1	60 blacks	
4/ 5/68	Duke		$1.60 minimum wage for U. workers	sit-in	4	600	
4/ 9/68	Michigan		discrimination	took over Ad Bldg.	1	100 blacks	
4/10/68	N.Y.U.		discrimination	presented demands	1		
4/23/68 to 5/22/68	Columbia		Morningside gym and IDA Association	school shut down	29	10,000	440 opposed 40 favor
4/24/68	Boston U.		discrimination	seize Bldg.6, present 14 demands	1	300	
4/26/68	Ohio State		discrimination	siege of building	3	75 black	
4/26/68	N.Y.C. area (800 campuses)		support for Columbia	strike	1	200,000	
5/ 1/68	S.U.N.Y.		support for Columbia	sit-in	1	40	
5/ 2/68	Princeton		students power	march	1	500	

A COMPARATIVE ANALYSIS OF CAMPUS TURMOIL (Cont'd)

Date	Reaction of Administration	No. of Students Arrested	Injuries to Students	Injuries to Authorities	On/Off Campus Police	Property Damage	Organizers	Long Term Effect	Sources
2/24/68									N.Y.T.
2/27/68									I.L.H.
2/28/68	use police	12			off				N.Y.T.
3/12/68	agreed to look into matter						Black Student Alliance	granted amnesty (May)	N.Y.T.
4/ 5/68							SAS		N.Y.T.
4/ 5/68									N.Y.T.
4/ 9/68	agreed to meet next week								N.Y.T.
4/10/68	pledges support						BAS	$1 mil. MLK scholarship fund set up; increase black enrollment	N.Y.Y.
4/23/68 to 5/22/68	4/24; request police on campus, 4/25; halt work. 4/30; send in 1000 police. 6/6; suspend 73 for 1 year	911	216		1000 police & National Guard	thousands of dollars	SDS, BSU, others	Pres. Kirk retires (August)	N.Y.T. I.L.H.
4/24/68	accepts 13 of 14 demands						UMOJA		N.Y.T.
4/26/68	accepts demands							24 later indicted	N.Y.T.
4/26/68		8	3						I.L.H.
5/ 1/68									N.Y.T.
5/ 2/68	will look into matter								N.Y.T.

A COMPARATIVE ANALYSIS OF CAMPUS TURMOIL (Con't'd)

Date	University	National Issue	Local Issue	Technique	Duration (in days)	No. of Students	Position of Faculty
5/ 6/68	Stanford		suspension of 7 students	take over Ad Bldg.	3	100	
5/ 8/68	Roosevelt		refusal to hire teacher	sit-in	8		
5/15/68	Chicago		discrimination	seize building	1	60 black	
5/17/68	Wisconsin	anti-Chase Bank		seize building	2	300	
5/20/68	Brooklyn		want more blacks & P.R.'s admitted	seize building	1	40	
6/ 4/68	Columbia		events of April–May	commencement walk-out	1	300	
6/12/68	Radcliffe	draft		arm bands at commencement	1	292	
8/ 6/68	N.Y.U.		appointment of "anti-semitic" dean	picket	1	15 Jews	

A COMPARATIVE ANALYSIS OF CAMPUS TURMOIL (Cont'd)

Date	Reaction of Administration	No. of Students Arrested	Injuries to Students	Injuries to Authorities	On/Off Campus Police	Property Damage	Organizers	Long Term Effect	Sources
5/ 6/68								suspension listed	N.Y.T.
5/ 8/68	45 students expelled	58						students get larger voice and amnesty	N.Y.T.
5/15/68	threaten suspension or expulsion								N.Y.T.
5/17/68									N.Y.T.
5/20/68	police	42			off		SFCAR		N.Y.T.
6/ 4/68									N.Y.T.
6/12/68									N.Y.T.
8/ 6/68									N.Y.T.

Social Change Through Confrontations in Social Movements

MUZAFER SHERIF

Pennsylvania State University
University Park, Pennsylvania

Whether the confrontation is on the campus, or is a black power confrontation, or a confrontation created by any other group of people in a state of unrest, it is always directed toward social change in the scheme of things—a change in the establishment. It is decidedly relevant, therefore, to consider social change as an essential framework for the main theme of confrontation.

When young people in a state of unrest insistently raise the question of relevance with regard to things as they are, the intent is social change, in general, and radical change in attitudes, in particular. For reasons that are readily understandable, the problem of social change is sorely neglected in the social sciences, in spite of its urgent relevance to the current social scene. The sociologist James S. Coleman[1] cogently summed up this point at a recent symposium devoted to the present state of social science:

> The current neglect (of social change) leads us to suspect that the whole discipline . . . has evolved toward the study of social statics, and becomes impotent in the face of change. Social change, social movements, conflict, collective behavior . . . are the underdeveloped

49

areas of social research. They are not only backward at present; they are not catching up.

Confrontations and Social Movements

Social movements serve as the clearest indicators of social problems. They are the best indicators of the simmering directions of social change, if not always the vehicle for change itself. Every social movement, small or large, engages in collective action (violent or nonviolent) such as demonstrations, protest meetings, boycotts, and even riots. In the social science literature, such public and out-of-the-ordinary modes of action are referred to as collective behavior. This is a more established term and, perhaps, more neutral term than confrontation. At the outset, three points have to be made about collective behavior before proceeding to an analysis of social movements:

1. The collective behavior aspect of a social movement may be sacrificial and heroic as well as beastly and destructive. The authors partisan to social movements made salient the heroic and sacrificial; the reactionary authors, the beastly and destructive.
2. The frequent label for collective flare-ups has been in terms of sickness or pathology. Such labels are misleading. Once a diagnosis is made in medical terms on social problems of such enormity, it erroneously appears that the solution is to call upon social "doctors" for a remedy with a relatively cheap price tag (say five to ten billion).
3. Flare-ups of collective behavior (violent or nonviolent) are inseparable parts or episodes of a social movement—but only *episodes* and not everything in the multifaceted pattern of a social movement.

With the foregoing, the focus of the theme has shifted from confrontation (or collective behavior) to social movements—for the locus of collective behavior is interaction in social movements.

Social Movements Form in Phases Over Time

What follows is a highly condensed account of a socio-psychological analysis of the rise of social movements which was developed over the last five years. For the sake of brevity, it must be presented in the form of a highly generalized statement without the empirical evidence documented elsewhere.[2]

Social psychologists have devoted much of their energy in recent decades to research on small groups. There is an overlap between the rise of a social movement and the formation of small groups, especially in their initial phase. The point of overlap is the human tendency, demonstrated time and again in empirical research, to move toward a new social formation when prevailing conditions prove to be exasperating and change for the better is not in sight.

However, in social movements we have to cope with large numbers of people, the wide geographic spread of events, and the characteristics of the status quo which the movement will confront sooner or later. The large number of individuals spread over wide stretches of geography raises special problems of organization and coordination.

A social movement makes sense only when considered as a developing formation over time, with ups and downs, through phases of unrest and angry protestation, of factionalism with diverse formulations of what lines of action are considered effective, to the phase of convergence on a more inclusive leadership and affirmative platform. In studying a social movement, or episodes of collective behavior within it, it becomes necessary to specify the point in time and formative stage in its natural history.

Needless to say, what are called here phases in a social movement are not mutually exclusive in time. The timing of the phases is not a matter of a year or two or the interval between two elections. Phases are retarded or accelerated by surrounding circumstances such as prosperity, peace, and solidarity within the system, or by war, depression, and within-system dissensions or divisions. In fact, they are inevitably affected by the entire scheme of relations within the country and by its particular place in the world scene.

The Motivational Base of a Social Movement

A social movement always rises from a motivational base that signifies social problems. Here, the phrase "motivational base" is used in a generic sense. The motivational base may consist of material destitution, such as hunger and miserable living conditions. It may consist of desperation caused by inhuman treatment, exploitation, racism, and colonialism. The motivational base may be disaffection or alienation arising from the divorce between what is preached day-in-and-day-out by those in authority and what is pursued relentlessly in actual practice. It may reflect the experience of relative deprivation, that is, a gap in the opportunities and privileges between groups that persists despite improvements in the plight of the under-privileged. For example, according to the U.S. Bureau of the Census,[3] the income gap between whites and nonwhites re-mained almost constant from 1947 to 1965. Human judgment is ever a comparison-making process. In this case, the under-privileged group compares its plight to that of the dominant group, and it is this comparison that determines whether its members perceive that their own group is at the level it should be.

The motivational base, fed by such social problems, is a *necessary* condition for the stirrings toward a social movement, but is not in itself *sufficient*. The necessary and sufficient conditions are still separated by the difficult human problems of converging on a *bill of gripes*, converging on a more inclusive leadership, and converging on an affirmative platform of changes along with strategy to chart the guidelines to action.

For the individual, reckoning with the problems of the motivational base by joining a social movement implies change. Such reckoning is a fateful step to take, for tearing one's self from the moorings of things as they are is a painful process, even when things are miserable. Shedding the ties and prestige symbols ingrained during a lifetime by a large number of people is not a feat to be achieved overnight. Such personal change can occur only when the motivational strain brings about alienation and, with it, repudiation of things as they are, at least of some prevailing institutions and practices. Temporarily, such alienation leaves the individual in a state of normlessness, which is a state of tension and instability not to be endured forever.

The end result is not doomed to be chaos, however. When a person is caught in a state of ambiguity, instability, and normlessness, the psychological tendency is toward some kind of stabilization, as numerous studies and experiments have shown. Thus, alienation and normlessness are conducive to active search for new alternatives. These may include switching to a new reference group, joining an ongoing movement, or throwing one's lot with thousands of others toward initiating a new movement.

The Initial Phase of a Social Movement

Even in the early years of a movement, there have to be heroes to be embraced, acceptable ideological formulas, and slogans. In spite of this, the most salient characteristic of a new movement in its initial phase is that its members are more clear about what they are *against* (what they reject) than what they are *for*. To take just one example, the student demonstrations in Paris in the spring of 1968 were more pronounced in what they were against, rather than in converging on a positive platform. Probably, at this early phase, it is a mistake to identify such negativism with particular doctrines, such as anarchism, even though a number of anarchists may be involved. A great variety of movements show this tendency to crystallize first on what they are against, while still divided into factions over specific changes to be instituted and strategy to be adopted.

Indeed, there are psychological bases for the strong, clear-cut rejection at this phase, related to the motivational base of the movement. In recent research measuring social attitudes, we have found it characteristic of highly committed persons to exhibit a very broad latitude of rejection; that is, to reject a very wide range of positions on the issue in question. In fact, the more involved the person is, the greater is his latitude of rejection compared to the range of positions acceptable to him (latitude of acceptance). Thus, in the early phase of a social movement, while various factions are not yet agreed on a latitude of acceptance, they do converge on a latitude of rejection, since these positions are those which they have come to recognize as responsible for their common plight.

We can begin to see why, during the initial years, the vehement expression of a *bill of gripes* serves as the rallying point for unity and solidarity among participants in a new movement. Thus, it would be misleading to view the frequent but sporadic flare-ups of collective behavior during this early phase apart from their locus in the pattern of the movement. No matter how emotional, and even irrational, such collective actions may seem when evaluated as isolated incidents by outsiders, their logic and function become understandable when viewed as part and parcel of a developing social movement. The vandalistic destruction of a valuable cargo of tea in the Boston harbor is just one example.

Convergence on an Affirmative Platform

Over time, the pattern of a developing social movement takes shape through the convergence of the motivational base and an ideological base, namely the crystallization of both a *bill of gripes* and a *platform of advocated changes and action strategies*, formulated by a coordinated leadership that arches over various factions. This convergence requires intellectual leadership that arches over various factions to translate the ideological premises into shortcut formulations and slogans that are relevant to ongoing actualities. It implies further differentiation of the roles and statuses of participants within the movement—in short, organizational solidification even in the face of factional disputes that almost invariably develop around platform, strategy, and action.

During the convergence phase, the occurrence or nonoccurrence of confrontations with the establishment, the relative frequency of collective action, and whether confrontations will be violent or nonviolent become a function of the platform and action strategy of the movement. At this point, the pattern of a social movement consists of much more than collective action and protest. Much of the activity involves planning, communication, office work, recruitment, and training, during which the character of collective behavior becomes more deliberately planned, coordinated, and staged.

Counterreaction to the Social Movement

The path of a social movement is not an open road strewn with rose petals. The moment the movement voices its protests and rejections in some form of collective action, it is confronted by counterreactions from the establishment, with coercive and even repressive measures. Countermovements arise both inside and outside of the establishment, both to justify and to execute repressive measures. This has been the predicament of almost every social movement of any scope, not excluding the black power movement and student unrest today.

The use of repressive force by the establishment or by countermovements quickly foments the dynamics of intergroup conflicts, which are by now well known.[4] In this case, the weight of power lies with the establishment, with the sense of victimization for the movement. On both sides, the latitudes of acceptance shrink still further, and latitudes of rejection expand. The chance that communication across partisan lines will have any effect, other than negative, approaches zero. Within the movement itself, the margin for tolerating deviation decreases, proportional to the risk that membership has come to entail.

Part of the challenge that social movements present to social science is the opportunity to study groups in formation, inter-

partisan encounters, attitude formation, and change within the
context of such events.[5] In the process, some of our cherished
notions are likely to be shaken. Take, for example, the prevailing conclusion in the research literature that little attitude
change is found in field studies, while laboratory studies yield
the greatest attitude change.

A recent report to the President by several Republican congressmen after a tour of university campuses includes an incident from the People's Park confrontation at Berkeley.[6] While
militant students demonstrated, two of the congressmen were
talking with moderate students nearby. At that moment, a
National Guard helicopter started spraying tear gas over the
campus. According to the congressmen, the effect on the non-
militant students was instantaneous—"they were radicalized
that moment." It is not merely a matter of whether research
is in the laboratory or in the field that determines whether there
will be attitude change or not.

The congressmen's report cited above illustrates another
common misconception, namely that the number of militant
members at a particular time is an adequate indicator of a
movement's viability and possible impact upon prevailing attitudes. The report noted that although militant students constitute a relatively small minority, there is a large proportion
of moderates who are similarly alienated by the establishment's
rigidity, and who take radical positions on specific issues, especially when repressive force is used.[7]

The significance of a movement as a force for change does
not depend merely on the number of its committed partisans
at a particular time, but upon how widespread the overlapping
social problems are that provide its particular motivational
base. As the political scientist Karl Deutsch[8] observed, an
assessment of the independence movement in the American
colonies in terms of its active supporters before the Revolution
would have been extremely misleading; they constituted no
more than a third of the colonial population. What counted
was the *potential* adherents of the movement—those affected
by the motivational base, but not yet active. Here the inde-

pendence movement outstripped those loyal to King George III by recruiting eight times the number of adherents.

In Summary and Conclusion

Pulling together the points made about the rise and stabilization of a social movement, a summary in six steps that also serve to characterize any social movement is as follows:

1. A social movement is a formative pattern of attempts toward social change that develops in phases over time.
2. It is initiated through interaction among people prompted by a motivational base that is fed by persisting social problems.
3. It is carried out by those directly affected and by others who throw their lot in with them.
4. It develops in phases through declaration of gripes and the formulation and proclamation of platform, which requires organization arching over its various factions.
5. It develops for the purpose of bringing about evolutionary or revolutionary changes, or of suppressing changes (in the case of countermovements).
6. Its efforts toward change are implemented through appeals to the public, slogans, symbolisms, agitation, recruiting, episodes of collective action, and confrontations with the opposition (strikes, rallies, resistance, boycotts, demonstrations, riots, insurrection, and so on).

In conclusion, if there is a single idea emphasized by this discussion, it is that confrontations of people with people—whether these be campus confrontations, black power confrontations, or confrontations by rising nationalisms—are parts of emerging social movements committed to change. Flare-ups of collective behavior in such confrontations are episodes within the pattern of the social movement, not events to be explained or dealt with apart from their cross-sectional properties at the time or from their particular phase of formation over time.

The occurrence of confrontations and associated collective
behavior can be meaningfully grasped and analyzed only in
the context of the temporal and cross-sectional pattern of the
social movement in question.

REFERENCES

1. J. S. Coleman, "Methods of Sociology," *Design for Sociology: Scope,
   Objectives and Methods*, ed. R. Bierstedt, American Academy of
   Political and Social Science, Monograph 9 (Philadelphia, 1969),
   pp. 86–114.
2. M. Sherif and C. Sherif, *Social Psychology* (New York: Harper and
   Row, 1969), Chapters 23–24.
3. U. S. Bureau of the Census, "Current Population Reports, 1967,"
   Series P-60, No. 53, 28 December, p. 44.
4. M. Sherif, *In Common Predicament: Social Psychology of Intergroup
   Conflict and Cooperation* (Boston: Houghton Mifflin, 1966).
5. C. Sherif, M. Sherif and R. Nebergall, *Attitude and Attitude Change*
   (Philadelphia: W. B. Saunders, 1965).
6. R. Evans and R. Novak, "Campus Revolt Hearings Changing Minds
   in House," *Pittsburgh Post-Gazette*, 31 May 1969.
7. *Boston Globe*, 13 July 1969.
8. K. W. Deutsch, "External Involvement in Internal War," *Internal
   War: Problems and Approaches*, ed. H. Eckstein (New York: Free
   Press, 1964).

Choosing the Right Analogy: Factory, Prison, or Battlefield

THOMAS C. SCHELLING

Harvard University
Cambridge, Massachusetts

Like everything else a university is unique, at least to those whose careers are involved in it. But when a unique institution suffers an unfamiliar ailment, the prognosis is up for grabs. The question is not, what *is* a university, but what is a university *like?*

Most of us, whatever side we are on, have an image in mind when thinking about "campus confrontation." Even the title of this session, "confrontation," can constrain our image and our vocabulary and, as a result, our thinking.

Students often have strong images. The SDS seems to believe that the occupation of University Hall at Harvard University last year was obviously justified—not merely justified, but *obviously* justified—so long as it is acknowledged that it was a political act. They further believe that to prove a political act it is enough to show that it had political results. The occupation did have political results. I have never understood why the political motives are a good excuse, but I am convinced that some students think so. Somewhere there must be an analogy so obvious to them that they are not aware that it is an analogy, and so obscure to me that I do not know how to refute the point if I am right that their analogy is wrong.

Analogies other than those I chose exist. There is that of a consumer movement, or of a church. I am not sure that mine are the closest analogies to campus violence; they are merely three that I have found suggestive. (Three is better than one because their very plurality insists that we are only exploring.)

A prison, in Erving Goffman's terminology, is a "total institution," like a nunnery or a boot camp or a mental hospital. The bargaining power of prisoners looks pretty small. They cannot recruit help from outside, communications are restricted, and they have no alumni association that looks out for them. There's not much they can withhold from the institution; much of their work is "make-work." They even have poor opportunities for violence because so much of the time they are locked up. But once in awhile they start some.

Often it begins in one of those moments of semi-freedom, like meal time. Once they become violent, there's not much they can do except occupy a building and take hostages. Once you have a building and some hostages, what do you do next? You announce your demands. But suppose you had no plans. You are like the fisherman with an enchanted sturgeon on his line: quick, make three wishes.

Early in the 1950's there had been few prison riots, and prisoners were poor at knowing what to demand once they had a building and some hostages. Gradually, over the first dozen riots, the grapevine worked and experience was shared, culture accumulated, and when prisoners had their buildings and their hostages they knew where to look for typewriters and mimeograph machines, how to draft demands, how to organize. Negotiations became stylized.

Put yourself in their position. What can you demand? Not anything that requires large amounts of money, because there's nobody available to command large amounts of money. You cannot call a legislature into session to change the budget because some cons have some hostages in a building. Demands have to be made on a tight time schedule. You can't stay there long, either working out your demands or making sure that agreements can be enforced.

One thing is easy to think of—amnesty. Once you're in the

building and the fun is over, safety is important, and amnesty is attractive, especially to the leaders, who typically formulate the demands. There is something else you may control: whom you negotiate with. You can specify that it be the warden or the governor or the publisher of a newspaper or someone from the Prison Reform Society or the chaplain. They don't *have* to comply, but you don't *have* to negotiate. You can often demand publicity. Sometimes you can demand subsequent investigation.

You can probably, in a hurry, think of particular individuals whom you would like fired, demoted, or punished. And often you need one demand—and can think of one—that is related in some way to the original outburst, so that it retroactively identifies the violence with your demands: better food, if it started in the dining hall; more exercise time, if it started in the exercise yard; better working conditions, if it started in a workshop. And there usually has to be at least one demand that dramatizes brutality or injustice, even nominal acceptance of which legitimizes the violence. This may be coupled with the demand that a particular individual be fired.

It is hard to get pledges that the demands will be kept once the hostages are released and the participants are back in their cells. This is one reason for publicity, for calling in referees.

It does not sound altogether different from occupied buildings on campus. My impression is that students who have occupied campus buildings converged fairly quickly on a standardized set of demands, more efficiently as successive occupations took place though different individuals were involved. Incidentally, the convergence of prisoner demands is strong evidence that "outside agitators" need not be present in order that a pattern become visible in the conduct of successive confrontations.

An important difference between the prison and the campus is that there is not much future in a prolonged confrontation in prison. If negotiations break down, or don't start, you've had it. It is hard to make a career out of failure there. There may be those on campus who have an interest in prolonging the violence or the occupation or the confrontation, who can look forward to careers built on the social disruption they have caused; there is no comparable career in prison martyrdom, yet.

Apparently in the prison situation, as in many campus situations, it is not the demands that motivate the violence, but the other way around. Confrontation generates demands. Violence was frequently unexpected by those who took part in it, even by its leaders. Afterwards the act has to be legitimized by being incorporated into the demands; the demands must project the image backwards, so that, whatever the violence was about, it is part of a movement and not an impromptu act.

Turn now to the factory. I wondered during our April uprisings what "student power" meant in the university. Is the "university community"—that paternalistic community in which students are junior members—on the way out? One of the first principles at Harvard, one that apparently has quite some appeal throughout the country, is that a student confrontation should in the first instance be treated as a university matter, within the "family," not for the police or the national guard, not for the courts. And when students are accorded "power," the power they are accorded is interwoven in the structure of the university.

This is not what American unions sought Unions in this country have been pretty clear about two things. They are not to be company unions—*not* to be part of the family. And they are not after membership on corporate committees; they do not want to be part of the corporate structure.

It will not altogether surprise me if this, something like the role of labor, becomes the role of students in the future. One reason it will not surprise me is that I expect it would be an effective role for them. They may be stronger outside the system, confronting it and negotiating with it, than joining it. Students might discover, as John L. Lewis discovered, that there is strength in industrial unionism, cutting across corporate lines. Do not let the university define the stage of your theater as this particular campus; if you are Harvard, combine with MIT, Boston, Northeastern, Tufts, Brandeis. There is strength in power and weakness in the disunity of your adversary. (And you may need money.)

Students may have discovered that added numbers, especially outsiders, provide immunity from disciplinary procedures, as well as experience and skill. At present the outsiders are advertised as "adventurers," veterans of skirmishes elsewhere, career dropouts, peripatetic confronters. Maybe the outsiders are going to be lawyers, researchers, negotiators, people good at formulating demands and negotiating, and immune to seduction by the power structure of any particular university.

Perhaps we should expect the development of appropriate instruments of coercion: nonviolent class boycotts, tuition strikes, the boycotting of ceremonies. Maybe they will discover techniques that beat violence from their point of view, and from ours.

At some stage the model of the National Labor Relations Act may become pertinent. What is the appropriate bargaining unit at a university: the medical school, the whole university, or all the universities in the metropolitan area? Who votes in the election of officers? Who certifies that the election was honest? What are the campaign rules? Who declares that the university has spoiled the election by providing public-relations assistance to some student candidate for office? When is a student union a company union? Will there be dues checkoff, a closed shop? Can unenrolled youths join the union and vote in the election of officers if they are willing to pay their dues or if they meet certain criteria for being "students"?

Out of all this might come a more conservative student movement than any that we have now. It took a decade or two for that to come out of industrial unionism, but I would expect it on campus, partly because there would be a career for more conservative students in this kind of campus political activity. (There might even develop some premium for dressing like the lawyer you hire or that you talk with across the table.) At most universities the majority student opinion is far less radical than the activities that hit the headlines. At most universities there's no way now that a silent majority, or even a silent large minority, can organize to express itself, to elect leaders and to bind themselves in negotiations. Evidently the more radical students want to avoid any large student movement that might, after a decade, become as conservative as Harry Bridges' International Longshoremen and Warehousemen's Union.

If this trend develops, there will arise the questions that arose within the CIO. Will a national student union be a political body or concern itself with the bread-and-butter issues of the university? My guess is that it would not end in bread-and-butter unionism, but be more like the CIO's Political Action Committee of the later New Deal days.

I have been talking about the students as "them," and find it harder to talk about the faculty. Who are "we" in this picture? We think of ourselves as elite members of a community that contains deans, lawyers, treasurers, clerks, typists, painters, carpenters and custodians. Maybe we're just part of the hired help, maybe a third party. I can squeeze something out of the analogy when I talk about students, but it leaves me stranded in thinking about the faculty.

So I turn now to the battlefield. I thought, when I contributed the title of this paper some months ago, that I was going to draw most of my insights from the battlefield. I was curious about the limits in war, about truces and how to maintain them, about escalation and de-escalation. I thought Israeli-Jordanian activity might offer an analogy for student-faculty activity. I did not mainly have guerrilla warfare in mind.

The asymmetry of guerrilla warfare is apparent here: almost everything that students do to us we cannot do to them (or it hasn't occurred to us). They can occupy our buildings, but they have no buildings that we care to occupy; they can boycott our classes, but teach no classes that we can boycott. They can interfere with a lot of what we do, but there's little that we can interfere in that they really want to do, especially if they enjoy the theatrics and we have to be careful not to make it easy for them by attempting reprisals in kind. "He who hath wife and child," Francis Bacon pointed out, "hath given hostages to fortune," or even he who hath fragile laboratory equipment, sensitive medical files, or a perishable manuscript. (Thank God for copying machines in the age of incendiarism.)

There is also a lack of organization and discipline on the part of the students, and one thing that may be learned from the history of the battlefield is that it is hard either to win or to lose a war if the other side is not organized. I am reminded of Winfield Scott's approach to Mexico City: he was told to take it easy or there might not be a government there to surrender when he took the place.

There are a few things on campus that are much like Vietnam, or most wars everywhere. One is the enormous importance attached to diplomatic recognition. It used to be said, "We will negotiate with the unions, but not as such." We will negotiate with the NLF, but not as much. We will negotiate with the black student political organization, but not "as such." "Our demands are not negotiable." The fear of legitimizing, dignifying, and recognizing the other side seems to be as much a principle on university campuses as it was in Algeria, Vietnam, or wherever contending factions in a civil war claim legitimacy.

Second is the role imputed to outside intervention. Non-university police come in, and it is like Americans or North Vietnamese coming into the country. In Secretary McNamara's language, it is "a wholly different war." On most university campuses the tradition of "conservatives" on both sides—the non-negotiators on both sides—is that there should not be any alien infiltrators or occupiers. The North Vietnamese must go home, the Americans must go home, the police must stay away, the Berkeley veterans have no business here, the French must stay out, the welfare mothers must stay out, the federal government must stay out, Stokeley Carmichael must stay out.

Third, almost everybody holds a domino theory, whichever side he is on, at Harvard or in Vietnam. The proceedings of faculty meetings are dominated by why we must not do this or that because of what it will lead to next time, the draft today and foreign policy tomorrow, black studies today and biology tomorrow, degree requirements today and tenure appointments tomorrow. It seems to be the same on the other side, the side of the radical students.

Fourth, and this happens too in military wars, the personal careers of leaders are involved in the policies they can accept and the decisions they can make. It may be that many, many more university presidents are going to discover what Lyndon Johnson did, that governments cannot reverse themselves. Governments resign, and let successor governments reverse themselves.

I was late arriving and walked into the middle of a talk, and the words that hit me were, "there can be no compromise of academic freedom with. . . . " I did not hear what it was that couldn't be compromised with. I am sure there are some things that cannot. The other side feels, too, that there can be no compromise. What makes it hardest for either side to get out of Vietnam, and what makes it hardest for either side to get out of a campus confrontation, is that issues in conflict are elevated—escalated—into moral principles. The trouble with moral principles is that they are hard to compromise, especially without personal admissions of turpitude. One of the troubles with saying that anything is a matter of high moral principle, that concessions would be unworthy of our traditions and unmanly in our behavior, is that if we yield and make the concession it is hard to recover. Life can go on, but it is less easy if we construe concession in advance as an admission of depravity and not merely of error. Ho Chi Minh and Lyndon Johnson converted what might have been a war over part of Southeast Asia into a test of mettle, of honor, of the future of two competing systems; and it is doubly difficult to disconfront.

A little less principle and a little more pragmatism, even less belief in a rigid domino theory, would be helpful. "No compromise" is a great battle cry but usually a poor strategy; "nonnegotiable demands" are the stock-in-trade of negotiators, but a dangerous faith.

I have tried to illustrate the "domino theory" with wooden dominoes. I have lined them up and struck the first one down; six fell and the seventh stood. I lined them up again and tried again, and after a few tries I could make all fall. It takes some care. Not all dominoes fall when one goes down. Not with wooden dominoes, probably not in Southeast Asia, probably not in university departments, nor even in a student movement. The weak version of the domino theory is incontestable; the absolute version is discredited on the living room floor.

II
Simulation of the Problem

Take a Longer Look

MILTON U. CLAUSER

Massachusetts Institute of Technology
Lincoln Laboratory
Lexington, Massachusetts

Before we resolve the conflict on campus, we may have to resolve some of the conflict within our own thoughts. The students have hammered away about the many things they see that need change. The reason we do not argue them down or ignore them is that we also see this very real need. I believe that we will be able to ignore the extremists and hammer down the anarchists when we see progress being made on changing the things that we believe need to be changed.

If there is such a consensus on the need for change, why is it that the needed action does not seem to be getting under way? In spite of a growing consensus for change there is no consensus for how to go about it, nor in what institutions to place our confidence for implementation. One day we flail Congress for not voting more billions to attack our favorite social ill, and the next we plead not to have our taxes spent on the Job Corps, OEO, the SST, or on runaway medical costs.

Perhaps not many of you would choose a university as the lead-off team for action. In our professional lifetime, the faculties and administrations have shown little interest or aptitude for public mission responsibilities. For the last twenty-five years, the emphasis has been on research and scholarly effort. Yet even now, almost every institution is reexamining its aims and goals. Let me quote from the questions raised by a committee preparing to reexamine the nature and purpose of an M.I.T. education:

Some of these people are urging their institutions to move toward a highly complex involvement with other areas of society. Others, including many faculty members, are concerned that the university which tries to attack society's ills will lose its strength in the basic academic disciplines. There is widespread concern that the running campus debate on so many complex issues threatens traditional research and scholarship by disturbing the serenity which many deem essential for creative thinking. A few insist that the problems of the moment are so pressing that most other activity should stop in order to attack these problems.

Those on one side of the argument have the convictions of their experience during the last ten to twenty-five years. Those on the other side are persuaded by our more immediate needs.

I find it most helpful to look back over a longer span of time and find that we are kidding only ourselves if we think that people have not faced such conflicts and such decisions before.

The priority has not always been to put research first, education second, and public service third. It was only a little over a century ago that we had forged the trails across the country to get to the gold fields of California. Then we faced the almost overpowering job of bringing this vast country to our use. There were railroads, mines, harbors, and water and sanitation systems to be built. The productive efforts of the great majority of people still had to be devoted to farming. Most of the universities stood aloof from the big job at hand. *Their* obligation was to educate men for leadership and letters. There were strong differences of opinion in the country as to whether this was the proper attitude and as to what the universities might be able to do to help a struggling nation.

But it was decided by those who prevailed that university help was necessary and the Morrill Act of 1862 *created* the land grant colleges needed to get the jobs done. Every state quickly had one or more colleges. When they started classes in agriculture, they realized they did not know what to teach. Let me quote from Professor Isaac Roberts of Iowa State Agricultural College (appropriately) in 1869:

I began to tell the students what I knew about farming. It didn't take long to run short of material and then I began to consult the

library. I might as well have looked for cranberries on the Rocky
Mountains as for material for teaching agriculture in that library.

So what did they do? Let me quote from the Office of Education Bulletin No. 9:

> The instructors, in agriculture particularly, realized that a body
> of scientific knowledge for the teaching of agriculture would have
> to be created, and they concentrated upon systematic experimental
> work, the results of which were utilized in the classrooms. With
> the development of agricultural research in the colleges . . . the
> possibility of the tremendous advantage of further experimentation
> on an extensive scale was soon realized. A number of colleges pro-
> ceeded to establish experiment stations at the college, the results of
> which were disseminated among the farmers through bulletins,
> circulars, and handsheets.

By the turn of the century, or shortly thereafter, the land
grant colleges had agents in almost ever county, extension
service to all farmers, representatives in the legislatures, aides
to the governors, and considerable power in the federal government. And of course, by this time, we were truly the *greatest
agricultural nation in the world.*

Remember, we are reviewing how an old problem was solved.
Here is what Dean Davenport gained from the experience:

> Perhaps the greatest single service rendered by the colleges in the
> early days was a sympathetic nursery for science and the scientific
> spirit. The colleges stood like a stone wall for the education of all
> classes and for putting knowledge to work for the direct betterment
> of society in all its interest, farmers particularly, as against the idea
> of an educated minority constituting aristocracy of learning and
> leadership.
> That public-supported institutions are by nature public-service
> institutions gradually developed as a logical corollary to the reason
> for their existence. The idea that research and education is mainly
> for the public welfare . . . gradually evolved as the logical if not
> the inevitable consequence of publically-supported institutions of
> higher learning.

A similar story could readily be told of how the civil engineers, the mechanical engineers, and the electrical engineers
of the land grant universities used their experiment stations to

help build the nation. By about 1920, the devotion of education and research to public service in the land grant universities had so greatly contributed to their physical and intellectual growth the other universities easily came to recognize them as peers.

The land grant universities were not the only ones to derive vitality and prestige from the composite of education, research, and public service. In the nineteenth century, American doctors were trained in a multitude of private schools, where the standards were set by the master's prejudices, and new knowledge was gained from practice. At the end of the century, some "young Turks" got a university medical school started at Johns Hopkins. By 1910, the Flexner Report brought the old into sharp contrast with the new. The force of the Flexner Report quickly brought school accreditation and state licensing of practitioners. Then, within a decade, the university medical schools were rapidly displacing the private schools. The teaching hospital which became a part of the university pattern was the means of bringing together education, research, and public service.

We may have some doubts today about how responsible the American Medical Association and the profession have been toward their stewardship during the last thirty years, but in the prior thirty years, full credit must go to the universities and their faculties which initiated such a remarkable change in the medical profession.

To round out our historical review, let me quickly remind you of the role that our universities played in World War II. In many, the priority shifted abruptly to public service at the start of the war. A large army of scientists devoted their full energies to the development of the atomic bomb. M.I.T. is still very proud of the work of the Radiation Laboratory in the development of radar. And there were many other projects which were undertaken by universities or by groups of professors on leave from universities.

After the war, the priority pendulum swung to research,

where it has been for the professional life of most of you. "Publish or perish" had come to be the byword, and many of the students had come to feel forgotten (remember?).

Now, more than a century after trails had been pushed through the mountain passes and the nation had faced up to the job of bending the frontier to its needs and its uses, we are faced with a strangely similar problem. In a sense, science and technology have made paths through the technical mountains. We have built automobiles, atomic bombs, televisions, and airplanes—we have gone to the moon. Now that we have mapped the technical frontier, we turn back and see the many things that we must better develop to our needs and our uses. *We* now must face up to the problems of traffic, pollution, education, medical care, and urban growth.

Over the last twenty-five-year span, the nation has not needed educational involvement and leadership in major public problems. But over a span of more than a hundred years, vital university involvement has been needed several times and has been found. And again, the universities are needed to help get a big job started!

Most of the nation's attempts at solving the major social problems, such as job training, compensatory education, welfare, medicare, and urban renewal, have been with such a broad and diffuse approach that there has been little feedback for evaluation and learning. The experience of the past shows how we should build from individual research results to more extensive experiments and then to critical-sized demonstration projects. In the process, education, research, and public service strongly support each other.

As a first step, many of my colleagues at M.I.T. have turned their individual research efforts toward some of our major civil problems. But they are coming to the realization that this is not enough. They do not foresee the means for action beyond their research which will make the Charles River any cleaner tomorrow, or will alleviate the traffic one whit tomorrow night, or make urban Boston any more dynamic! The university involvement requires a bigger push, a more extensive and concerted effort, if it is to prototype workable solutions and to couple learning and evaluation to experimentation.

How big a commitment might a university group have to undertake in order to bring its efforts up to critical mass in size? The money which was going into agricultural experiment stations was a fraction of a percent of the gross farm product of the country. From experience with a number of major military systems, it required about one percent of the production deployment expenditure rate to bring the system concept to a convincing stage of demonstration. In today's world, it is conceivable that our nation may have to spend many billions of dollars per year for a decade or more to effect the advances we desire in such areas as pollution, traffic, medical care, and vocational education. The university groups which will help to tackle these problems may have to expand their research efforts to experimental programs requiring some tens of millions of dollars each per year. Admittedly, it is difficult to make such predicitions when the programs will have to try to satisfy many parties with such diverse interests.

Why should the universities be called upon to make commitments of this magnitude? There is both a simple answer and a complex answer. The simple answer is that I see sufficient similarity between the situations of a century ago, a half-century ago, and of the 1970s to say that the universities are needed for the same reasons they were needed in the past and they have the same obligations. Let me try to shorten the longer answer. First, a part of the solution is *doing*, but maybe a bigger part is *learning*. Second, the universities seem to be the one place where the job can be approached most objectively. They do not have an empire to build or a gimmick to sell. Third, the universities can offer a great breadth of expertise and interest, and we have come to recognize how complex are most of our social problems.

Will the great universities stand aside today as did those of a century ago and require that new organizations be created to learn how to make the changes that must be made? Or will some put their shoulder to the load as several did a half-century ago for medical care and medical education?

I believe that history puts the heavy burden of proof on those who say that public service detracts from the opportunity for scholarly achievement. The preoccupation of the land grant colleges with experimentation and public service for agriculture and engineering made both the universities and the nation great.

And a half-century ago, it was the combination of education, research, and public service which transformed our medical practice from the style of the medicine man to a highly respected profession and made the university medical schools famous.

The war R & D of a quarter of a century ago laid the cornerstone of the so-called scientific revolution, and the nation then proceeded to invest a sizeable fraction of its budget in research at the universities on the conviction that such research would pay off in public dividends.

We now may quarrel with whether the right goals were chosen, and whether, after the goals had been attained, those who had benefited most continued to serve the public interest, but it is difficult to argue, based on experience, that involvement in current national problems inhibits or detracts from creative thinking.

In summary, let me suggest, particularly to university colleagues, that one of the steps needed to resolve the conflict on the campus is to resolve our own conflict on what part of the action we will accept. Recalling the quotations from those who have faced the alternatives: Do we want to avoid "disturbing the serenity which many deem essential for creative thinking"? Or do we want "the colleges (to stand) like a stone wall for . . . putting knowledge to work for the direct betterment of society in all its interests"?

Gaming and Planning for Campus Crises

MARTIN SHUBIK

Yale University
New Haven, Connecticut

I have been working at Yale with a class of about fifteen graduate and undergraduate students in a course on group decision theory. Our project has been to build an operational game on campus crises. The purpose has been more to teach them how to go about studying phenomena, such as campus crises, and to examine the use of operational gaming than it has been to solve the burning question of the moment.

In particular, I want to contrast two aspects of operational games. One is the war game where the basic assumption is that there is a well-defined polarization of interests and that is the way things are going to be. The other is what you might call the community operational game where an important part of the experience is to improve understanding among the participants and, if anything, to lessen polarization. Our game is in the latter category.

As a matter of fact, I don't even know whether we will run the game we have constructed. I am not particularly worried about this because, in my opinion, the major value of operational games is gained in building them. The construction of the game by a group is probably more valuable than the playing of the game. In certain very specific situations, it may be the other way around. But in this case I doubt it.

In particular, we went through the following steps. First, the construction of reasons for an incident and then the description of the incident. This exercise took a great amount of time for fairly obvious reasons. It is always unclear which comes first, the reason or the incident.

The next step was to make a list of the actors. To prepare the scenario, we used a modified Delphi process to select reasons and incidents from the list we had prepared. We then selected actors and wrote actors' positions. Then came the actual construction of a preliminary scenario. After this, we reverted to the consideration of the major reasons for difficulties on the campus. This raised the question, What does one mean by the university and its role in society? In the discussion back and forth, it became apparent that the perception of university goals was enormously varied.

Tom Schelling likes analogies and, for that matter, so do I. However, one has to be fairly careful in the use of analogies since often they merely confuse the issue. Frequently, the more picturesque the analogy, the easier it may mislead. Having given my warning, let me note a couple of the analogies that came up in our discussion.

The university . . . the word university these days is used in the same way as is the word *automobile*. But in the automobile business, there is the production line that is producing Volkswagons and there is the production line that is producing Rolls Royces. The market, the technology, and many other features in those production lines are very, very, very different. I do not know the answer to much of the malaise in our current university environment but one might start by looking at the system implications of the considerable change in mass higher education over the last twenty-five years starting from the end of World War II and the introduction of the GI Bill.

At the present moment in our seminar, we are considering the question, How many models are there or should there be? Certain universities are elitist institutions. Does somebody want to make a lengthy case for or against this? If one has an elitist university, that might be considered as University Mark I.

There may be Mark II to Mark XX before we have enough differentiation among the universities.

For reasons that I still am not completely satisfied with, we love to dichotomize. I wonder how much different our thinking would be if we always trichotomized. The dichotomous treatment of problems came up in questions concerning the university and its role as an agent of social change.

There was also the question of the university's role in adult education. The question is really twofold. First, is the university a multiproduct industry? Suppose you happen to answer that question negatively and say that it is a single-product industry. Then how many models of that product should it be dealing in? If you want to constrain it to say undergraduate and graduate education, do you want to have city colleges, teachers' colleges, ivy league, big tens, polytechnics, and others?

What has this question to do with the gaming of campus crises? Just in the process of trying to construct this operational game, several interesting things happened. During the first couple of sessions, there was a fair amount of heat. There were a number of students who had strong feelings and opinions (and I suspect they still do). But somehow, in the process of using the methodology of building on operational game, we apparently established a degree of professionalism. And to some extent (at least at the level of discourse), we established a considerable de-escalation in the level of emotion in trying to analyze critical problems.

Returning to detail, the list of the actors included the SDS, the president's office, university police, junior and senior faculty, news media, New Haven police, black students at Yale, community groups, state administration, Governor Dempsey, ad hoc student groups, graduate student senate, university non-faculty employees, New Haven citizens, New Haven administration from the mayor's office, alumni, the federal and the state police, the city planning office, and several others. The students took these categories and wrote position papers after the class had selected the incident and the scenario. They wrote their position papers after a reasonable amount of research. I must note that it is pleasant to be involved in an educational process where you stand at least a sporting chance of learning as much from the session as the students are learning and also have the feeling that the students may be learning something at the same time. This group effort had that property.

The class is presently preparing the final scenario and the game control. When we finish that, which will be fairly soon, the question will come up as to whether or not we actually play the game. I am not sure that we will. One of the reasons why I'm not sure is that I have contributed to the effort a metascenario—a precognitive scenario—and it goes like this:

A professor, an expert in gaming, organizes his class to run an operational game on campus confrontation. Actors are invited from the outside. Several members of the community show up. Several SDS students show up incognito, manage to incense some of the participants in the course of the game playing, provoke violence, and—*voilà!*

Although we do not know whether we will run the game, it is not really important to do so because the major value has already been obtained in its construction.

I find that the use of gaming in this manner can serve the purpose of lessening polarization and increasing understanding. It has been an effective way of involving a fair number of students. I would like to try it again with even more. The project managed to get students into a structured situation where they were not trying to win debating points from each other. There was a great amount of good professional work accomplished in writing position papers and in presenting the final position papers. I perceive (although I can give you no useful measures at this moment) a distinct broadening of everybody's understanding, including my own, and a distinct lessening of the tensions involved in exploring an explosive topic.

Another point that should be noted concerns the validation of the use of games. I want to discuss this because those who have been involved in gaming know how infinitely hard it is to construct measures of validity for either operational games or for experimental games. In the case of war games, one of the reasons why it is so hard to establish measures of validity is that the stated purpose has nothing to do with the real purpose. A classical example of that was given by Roberta Wohlstetter in her book on Pearl Harbor. The Japanese War College had a large war game prior to Pearl Harbor. If one takes a look at it, one would observe that it was more a method of trapping all three of the top Japanese services, plus the Japanese diplomatic corps, in one room while the army told them the way things were going to be, than it was an operational game. That was basically the form it took.

A conventional attempt at validation of the Japanese war game would have been worthless. This is especially interesting because the Japanese navy had fits during that war game with the proposition that they should expose virtually their whole carrier force in an attack on Hawaii. Had we been just a little more alert, I think they would have had good reasons for their fits.

There are many measures for validating a game. The validation of the game that I have been working on is different from many. The students and the faculty are learning how to produce abstract models by constructing the game. Whether they play it or not may be interesting, but it is not necessarily where the action is. The learning by building the game is where the value is.

There is a story about what are reputed to be Gertrude Stein's last remarks. She was going for an operation from which she would not survive. As she was about to be wheeled into the operating room, she knew that she had better say something worthwhile. She tried, "What is the answer?" Alice B. Toklas looked at her and observed that the line was not particularly notable. So she thought again and said, "Well then, what is the question?"

III
International Conflict
Analysis and Simulation

Some Problems of International Conflict Analysis

E. RAYMOND PLATIG*

U.S. Department of State
Washington, D. C.

Since the advent of the nuclear age we have become accustomed to thinking of this great globe itself as one large living system. This trend in our thought and conception stems
not just from the horrendous consequences associated with
explosive nuclear power but from other developments as well.
Thus, we have become aware of the large scale, if not world
wide, implications of atmospheric and water pollution. We
have come to see ourselves as the space ship "earth" not only
because we can view ourselves from the moon but also because
space communications and sensors carried by earth satellites
make it possible for us—at least for some purposes—to reach into
all corners of the earth.

This view of the earth as one large living system has had
its impact on the way in which we think about international
politics. It is now fairly common to think of the international
political system, global in scope, as a subsystem of a larger
international social system with still other intertwined sub-
systems such as an international economic system, a system of
international law, an international scientific and technological
system, and so forth. Such grand thoughts lead quickly to the

*The views expressed in this article are those of the author and are not to be
construed as expressing the official position of the Department of State.

87

further thought that conflict anywhere in the international system immediately has its repercussions and implications for the entire system. Certainly there is some historical evidence to support that view. Very discernible trends in the increasing interdependence of peoples around the globe suggest that the sensitivity of the whole system to conflict anywhere within itself is bound to increase.

These various trends, thoughts, and fears have sent a number of scholars and others on the search for an adequate model of the international system. The more ambitious are in search of a model that would make it possible to monitor the growth, decay, and development of the forces which underlie the emergence of critical imbalances in the global living system. This search is based upon a number of hopes or assumptions (1) that we can identify the critical forces and factors, (2) that we can validate our identifications by systematic research into past and current cases, (3) that we can come to understand the dynamics of the interrelationships of these forces and factors, (4) that we can develop reliable current indicators and measures such that we can trace the unfolding of these forces and factors and their dynamic interrelationships, (5) that we can thereby predict where trouble is brewing, and (6) that we can therefore take early action to head off trouble or minimize its impact.

Does the promise of conflict avoidance held out by such a system of analysis and control make its development a matter to which we should give high priority in the allocation of resources? I know of no cost benefit analysis that has been done to arrive at an answer to this question. The way in which some people spend their own time either as researchers or in the effort to develop research resources would indicate to me that they have answered the question in the affirmative. It is not the kind of question that such institutions as the U.S. Department of State are accustomed to posing for themselves. Most of those outside the Department of State who prefer an affirmative answer are convinced that those inside the Department of State prefer a negative answer. The reasons usually given are somehow related to the proposition that foreign affairs practitioners tend to be humanists rather than scientists and don't want to see scientific developments put them out of business.

Without taking up the cudgels for either the Department of State or the foreign service I would like to spell out some of the problems which I personally detect in this approach to the analysis of conflict in the international system.

I propose to discuss these problems under the following two major headings.

The Philosophy of Science

There has been raging for some time now within the social sciences a debate about their scientific nature and content. It has been a far-ranging and often confused debate—one difficult to characterize or summarize. It is thus too facile to say that the debate has centered around the poles of *rigor* and *relevance,* or around the poles of *abstraction* and *real life,* though those are key terms in the debate and at least indicative of its nature. The debate has become heated in the last few years with the emergence in the various social sciences of a growing group of concerned activists. They have brought new meanings to the terms *relevance* and *real life* but have not really altered the basic terms of the debate. They have, however, forced some rethinking and some rather substantial concessions from those who, in the past, have taken their stand at the poles of rigor and abstraction, those who have been known in the trade as the behavioralists.

One indication of the extent of the concessions is the address David Easton delivered to the American Political Science Association.[1] His paper makes clear that his heart is very much that of a behavioralist and that his devotion to a basic science approach to his field is undiminished. He appears to interpret the demand for relevance and action as rooted more in the crises of our time than in nonbehavioral intellectual premises. He, too, is impressed with the horror of the crises and seeks "a strategy that will enable us to respond to the abnormal urgency of the present crises and yet preserve" the traditions of basic science. To accomplish this, Professor Easton suggests "an optimizing strategy in which there is some apportionment of resources for the long run as against the short run, just in case we are not in fact dead." This invitation to a reapportionment of resources is indeed a major concession by the behavioralists to the relevant activists; whether it can be implemented in a way to satisfy the activists remains to be seen.

There are also signs of an even more fundamental rethinking of the tenets and claims of behavioralism. A serious effort along these lines is contained in a paper by Bert A. Rockman of the University of Michigan, a paper entitled "A 'Behavioral' Evaluation of the Critique of Behavioralism."

After dismissing what he considers the more extreme and unreasonable critiques of behavioralism, Professor Rockman goes on to summarize five ways in which "the possibilities of scientific revelation" have been overstated by the behavioralists.

> First, there is the assumption that men of objective bent can repair to the gospel of the data and eschew ideology. Yet it is inevitable that behavioral science will become a vehicle of ideology. For the methods of science are not automatic; instead, they reflect the daily conscious and unconscious research decisions and operationalization that color the end product of the research. Perhaps explicit ideology is preferable to false consciousness.
>
> Second, there is a tendency to develop jargonistic categories of analysis that are so broad and ambiguous that they are of little use for empirical analysis. This is especially the case among those addicted to systems analysis models.
>
> Third, there is a kind of narrow self-promoting pompousness that too often assumes that only social scientists, and only a very special breed of these, have anything worth contributing to political knowledge.
>
> Fourth, it is frequently assumed that maintaining value neutrality in social research can be accomplished if researchers consciously place their values to one side. While a self-consciousness as to personal values is helpful, the processes of ideological contamination are not only quite subtle but also continuously affect the formulation and interpretation of research through the snowballing of minor operational decisions.
>
> Finally, the presumption that scientific discovery and theory are cumulative has long been a cherished component of the behavioral belief system. Nonetheless, the diversity of analytic levels, the variety of conceptual arrays, and the instability of attitudes and behaviors all

lend some credence to an occasional doubt regarding the unity of scientific knowledge. Anticipating the emergence of some general thories that will tie together all of the bits and pieces and transform all of the nonlineraities is likely to be in vain. While it would be nonsense to assert that all research is unrelated, it would also be well to recognize that all social knowledge is temporally, culturally, ideologically, and technically constrained. All of these factors serve to impose serious limits upon our ability to cumulate knowledge.[2]

They constitute fundamental philosophical problems which it one, seem to me to cast grave doubts on the feasibility of the kind of system of analysis and control I mentioned at the outset. They constitute fundamental philosophical problems which it would be foolish to ignore in the rush to build large-scale models of the international system in the search for prediction and control of conflict in the system. Such models may serve highly intriguing and provocative intellectual and heuristic purposes; they may even generate important increments to our ability to estimate and influence, but the belief that they will eventually permit reliable prediction and control of conflict in the international system remains an article of faith.

The Political Problems

There is a second category of problems in this approach to the analysis of conflict which I shall call simply political. The fundamental political question is, *Who* is going to control *what* conflicts in the international system? I assume that this is a question which surfaced in one or more forms in the sessions on "campus confrontation." If it is true that knowledge is power, then the question "Knowledge for whom?" becomes a political question. Student groups have shown an appreciation of the importance of that question by resisting certain social science studies of campus violence conducted on behalf of what the students consider to be the educational establishment.

This politicalization of research and analysis of conflict, evident on the domestic scene, is even more in evidence on the international scene. For in the international system the authority of established power is even more tenuous and the exercise of power even more suspect than in most domestic systems. Thus, for example, recent statements to the effect that the United States wishes to play "world policeman" are not designed to commend it for its civic mindedness but rather to accuse it of arrogating to itself a power *vis-a-vis* the conflicts within and between other nations for which it has no authority.

It is a political maxim of long standing that power is tempted to arrogance and it is incumbent upon a great power in the international system to check itself in this regard. What is perhaps not as readily recognized is that knowledge and knowledge seekers can also be tempted to arrogance. I do not have in mind the academic possessors of some irrefutable scientific but partial truth who sometimes take a belittling attitude toward practitioners mired to their neck in the intractable richness of reality. That is a form of arrogance, but not the one that concerns me here. Rather I have in mind the easy assumption of some social and behavioral scientists who, because they feel the need for certain data to develop their models, believe that others at home and abroad should gladly cooperate in supplying the needed data.

Even though I will take a back seat to no one in preferring knowledge to ignorance, I have personally been appalled by some of the data-gathering instruments I have seen circulated by private researchers to selected members of the Washington bureaucracy. Some of these instruments probe attitudes and beliefs which no sensible man would think of sharing with any but the closest of confidants. Others pose delicate questions about matters which no one aware of a variety of foreign sensitivities would consider fit subjects for public comment by a range of government officials.

When similar instruments are projected by American researchers into foreign societies, there are often added difficulties stemming from the way in which cultural norms and local rivalries affect the perception of the data-gathering enterprise in general and assign importance to specific classes of data in particular. From the point of view of the scientific analysis of conflict in the international system, the need for a vast and varied array of social seismometers located around the globe may seem logical beyond dispute. From the point of view of persons and groups caught up in actual or potential conflict situations, such instruments are more likely to be seen as annoying, if not threatening, foreign intrusions.

My point is simply that those interested in the analysis, prediction, and control of conflict in the international system can no more ignore these fundamental political problems than they can the fundamental philosophical problems mentioned earlier. Indeed, it seems to me that both kinds of problems are so rooted in the basic human condition that we would do well to eschew the massive break-through aspiration that so frequently characterizes scientific enterprise and focus on the possibility of more modest gains.

In that spirit, and to avoid leaving the impression that I see only insuperable problems standing in the way of improving our ability to deal with conflict in the international system, permit me to mention what appear to me as hopeful signs and modest gains.

First of all, the Department of State is now in the advanced stages of designing a substantive information system which five years from now should provide a greatly improved means of handling the vast flow of information which inundates the department. The system being developed has five major objectives:

1. to give the user more incoming *information* relevant to his responsibilities while reducing the flow of *documents* that contain little information of use to him
2. to reduce the waste of time and energy in retrieving documents already received
3. to identify new sources of information (in other U.S. agencies and academic institutions, for example) and make them readily accessible
4. to make information available in new and more useful forms, beyond the traditional documents
5. to make available new tools for the manipulation of

information so that relationships can be postulated, evaluated, and communicated to other people.[3]

A second hopeful sign is that the department is taking an increased interest in longer-range projective research and analysis for policy planning and program evaluation purposes. A small group is now at work exploring some of the recently developed research methodologies and analytical techniques which have potential applications to these and related purposes. The objective is to identify those techniques which the department itself should import and tailor to its specific needs. The possibility of employing these techniques in the future will be enhanced by installation of the substantive information system, which is to be computer based. The system is being so designed that department officers can have a capability for the creation of special information and data files.

> Designed and maintained for users, these files will free information from documents and make it easily available for specific purposes. Some potential special files of this sort include *fact files* on political parties, national accounts, treaties, etc.; *chronologies*, particularly useful in crisis situations, where the *order* of events often assumes importance; *precedent files*, showing what *we* did, or what *they* did, in the last similar situation; and *policy statement files*, comprising the word-for-word texts of important pronouncements by national and international leaders.[4]

It takes little imagination to see how such a capability could be used to improve our efforts to understand and cope with conflicts in the international system.

Third, despite the fact that there are some extraordinary strains in government-academic relations these days, I see some very promising developments emerging in the academic community. Social and behavioral scientists generally are showing increased sensitivity to the value frameworks within which they work and to the foreign sensitivities on which their work often impinges. Among the results is an increased awareness of the practical implications of what they study, under whose auspices, for what purposes, and whose benefit. Another result is increased attention to the desirability of developing research capabilities in other nations and of cross-national collaboration in important research projects.

Most encouraging of all is a snowballing interest in problem-oriented research. It has long seemed to me that those interested in theory and method in the social sciences have short-changed themselves as well as society by avoiding real-life problems which are too complex to fit within the confines of their abstract theory and too imprecise to be encompassed by their indicators and measures. Problem-oriented research requires that one step well outside the bounds of his discipline, but, in the process, the discipline itself can be enriched by demonstrations of the strengths and weaknesses of its theory and methodology. Thus, I find it an encouraging sign that the National Science Foundation, the National Academy of Sciences, and the various disciplines are showing a greater interest in applied research. Again, the paper by David Easton (referred to earlier) provides an example of this trend. In it he issues an urgent call "for the systematic examination of the tasks involved in transforming our limited knowledge today into a form far more consumable for purposes of political action."[5]

These developments come during the time of a president who has declared his belief that "neither the Department of State nor of Defense has a monopoly on all wisdom"[6] and when the Secretary of State has urged the department to manifest an expanded openness to "creative and innovative ideas, as well as thought-out dissent."[7] If the disciplines follow through on their declared interest in applied research, it is not unreasonable to hope that we are on the edge of an era when both new excitement and new effectiveness will be brought to the analyses which precede the formulation of public policy for dealing with conflict in the international system. We would deceive ourselves if we did not anticipate that it will also be an era of intellectual and ideological tensions. Can we hope that we will learn to work these out in seminar and conference rooms, and through serious study and informed debate, rather than in the street and at the barricades?

REFERENCES

1. David Easton, "The New Revolution in Political Science," mimeo-graphed (Presidential Address delivered at the Sixty-fifth Annual Meeting of the American Political Science Association, New York City, September 2–6, 1969), 19 pp.
2. Bert A. Rockman, "A 'Behavioral' Evaluation of the Critique of Be-havioralism," mimeographed (Delivered at the Sixty-fifth Annual Meeting of the American Political Science Association, New York City, September 2–6, 1969), pp. 4–5.
3. "Modernizing State Department Information Processes," *Far Horizons* (September 1969), p. 4.
4. *Ibid.*
5. Easton, "New Revolution," p. 9.
6. *The New York Times*, September 20, 1968, p. 33.
7. "A Message from the Secretary," *Department of State News Letter*, no. 102 (October 1969), inside cover.

Cross-National Analysis of Political Violence

IVO. K. FEIERABEND

San Diego State College
San Diego, California

The purpose of this presentation is to outline a program of comparative, cross-national study of political violence and aggression pursued by Rosalind Feierabend, Betty Nesvold, and myself.[1] Three aspects of our endeavor are outlined: cross-national data collection, theoretical analysis, and some of the global patterns of internal political turmoil that emerge from our studies.

We are interested in political aggression and violence as it occurs within all nations. Violence can be directed against officeholders, which we designate as civil strife or political instability. Examples of specific instability events are demonstrations, riots, assassinations, coups d'etat, and revolutions. Violence and aggression are also initiated by officeholders, and this we call political coerciveness. Typical coerciveness events are arrests, imprisonments, executions, banning of opposition parties, censorship, and others. Finally, there is aggression between groups in the political system; events of ethnic, religious, and racial tension are examples.

These three general types of political violence guide our collection of data. We have accumulated a Cross-National Data Bank of Political Instability Events, a Cross-National Coerciveness Data Bank, and a Cross-National Minority Tension Data Bank.[2] The information is coded and stored on Hollerith cards. It derives from a variety of sources, ranging from a simple chronicle of events such as yearbooks of encyclopedias, or news-culling services such as Deadline Data on World Affairs, to more detailed sources such as *The New York Times* and monographic case studies in the literature of comparative government.

In our earlier collections, we usually concentrated on a sample of eighty-four nations which were independent states in 1945. Now we are collecting information for dependent as well as independent nations. The time span of our collection varies from periods of a few years to more than twenty years at mid-twentieth century (1945–1967). As already suggested, many specific conflict events are recorded in the data banks: imprisonments, confiscations, coups, martial laws, falls of cabinets, resignations and dismissals of officeholders, executions, exiles, police actions, demonstrations, riots, strikes, assassinations, acts of sabotage and terrorism, revolts, civil wars, and other acts of political aggression. In the latest collections, we name more than one-hundred conflict variables. These events, furthermore, are described in some detail on the Hollerith cards. In what country did the event take place? How long did it last? Where did it take place? What issue was involved that triggered the event? What group participated in the event? Who was the target and who the initiator of the aggressive impulse? How many people were involved? How many people were injured or killed? Additional information is also specified about each event of violence.

From this data base, we have developed several methods of looking at the complex universe of violence. Perhaps the simplest way is to ascertain the frequencies of these events that took place within the many nations during specified periods of time. Such frequency counts can include a single name event or combine several or all events. Table 1 is an example of such a procedure. It could be labeled as a cross-national assassination map. Countries are rank-ordered by counting the assassination events from 1948–1967. Cuba stands on top of the list

TABLE 1

Frequencies of Assassinations
(1948 – 1967)

Country	No. of Assassinations	Country	No. of Assassinations
Bulgaria	0	Mexico	3
Chile	0	Paraguay	3
China (Taiwan)	0	Thailand	3
Denmark	0	Union of So. Africa	3
East Germany	0	Turkey	4
Finland	0	Burma	5
Honduras	0	Cyprus	5
Iceland	0	Czechoslovakia	5
Ireland	0	Greece	5
Luxembourg	0	Haiti	5
Netherlands	0	Indonesia	5
Norway	0	Iraq	5
Peru	0	Nicaragua	5
Poland	0	Pakistan	5
Romania	0	Panama	5
Sweden	0	Cambodia	6
Switzerland	0	Jordan	6
United Kingdom	0	Malaya	6
Uruguay	0	Colombia	7
U.S.S.R.	0	Dominican Republic	7
Austria	1	Ghana	7
Belgium	1	Syria	7
Canada	1	India	8
Hungary	1	Argentina	9
Libya	1	Bolivia	9
New Zealand	1	Japan	9
Sudan	1	Laos	10
Afganistan	2	Brazil	12
Albania	2	Guatemala	12
Australia	2	Lebanon	12
Ceylon	2	Venezuela	12
Costa Rica	2	Egypt	14
El Salvador	2	France	14
Ethiopia	2	Philippines	15
Liberia	2	Tunisia	16
Portugal	2	United States	16
Saudi Arabia	2	Morocco	17
Spain	2	Iran	19
West Germany	2	Korea	20
Yugoslavia	2	Cuba	28
China (Mainland)	3		
Ecuador	3		
Israel	3		
Italy	3		

with twenty-eight assassinations. These counts include attempted as well as plotted and successful assassinations.

It is tempting to comment at length on the findings in this table. Instead, let us only notice the position of the United States. Together with Tunisia, this country is the fifth in the world most prone to this kind of political aberration. Indeed, one may wonder why it is that the United States did not find its way to the group of modern, highly industrialized, Western, democratic nations where assassinations seem the exceptional occurrence. The United States and also France appear in this table as the mavericks.[3]

Beyond frequency counts of instability events, we have used other techniques in trying to identify global patterns of violence. Among them is factor analysis. It yielded several dimensions (factors) of conflict behavior, that is, clusters of violence variables that frequently are associated and are quite unrelated to other such clusters.[4] We have also developed several scaling instruments of violent events ranging from simple construct-validity scales to more complicated ones. Often we use six- or seven-point scales where each successive point of the scale denotes a more intense form of violence. For example, dismissals or resignations of officeholders are assigned a scale position of number 1; peaceful demonstrations, peaceful strikes, or martial law, a scale position of 2; riots and assassinations, position 3; large-scale arrests, imprisonments, large-scale riots, position 4. Revolts are included in scale position 5, while full-scale civil war, the pinnacle of political violence, is located at scale position 6.[5]

Similar scales were developed to measure the other types of aggression: coerciveness, minority tension, and also international aggression.[6] Sometimes not just events are rated, but entire situations within countries, to estimate infringements of civil rights, associational freedoms, tolerance of political opposition, restrictions of suffrage, and other coerciveness variables. The Coerciveness Data Bank includes some seventy variables, with information for eighty-four countries available for every year of a twenty-two-year period (1945–1966). Using

TABLE 2

Frequency Distribution of Countries in Terms of Relative Political Stability

Stability ← 0	1	2	3	4	5	6 → Instability
New Zealand 000	Norway 104	West Germany 217	Tunisia 328	France 499	India 599	Indonesia 699
	Netherlands 104	Czechoslovakia 212	Great Britain 325	Union of So. Af. 495	Argentina 599	Cuba 699
	Cambodia 104	Finland 211	Portugal 323	Haiti 478	Korea 596	Colombia 681
	Sweden 103	Romania 206	Uruguay 318	Poland 465	Venezuela 584	Laos 652
	Saudi Arabia 103	Ireland 202	Israel 317	Spain 463	Turkey 583	Hungary 652
	Iceland 103	Costa Rica 202	Canada 317	Dom. Republic 463	Lebanon 581	
	Philippines 101		United States 316	Iran 459	Iraq 579	
	Luxembourg 101		China (Taiwan) 314	Ceylon 454	Bolivia 556	
			Libya 309	Japan 453	Syria 554	
			Austria 309	Thailand 451	Peru 552	
			Ethiopia 307	Mexico 451	Guatemala 546	
			East Germany 307	Ghana 451	Brazil 541	
			Denmark 306	Jordan 448	Honduras 535	
			Australia 306	Sudan 445	Cyprus 526	
			Switzerland 303	Morocco 443		
				Egypt 438		
				Pakistan 437		
				Italy 433		
				Belgium 432		
				Paraguay 431		
				U.S.S.R. 430		
				Nicaragua 430		
				Chile 427		
				Burma 427		
				Yugoslavia 422		
				Panama 422		
				Ecuador 422		
				China(Mainland) 422		
				El Salvador 421		
				Liberia 415		
				Malaya 413		
				Albania 412		
				Greece 409		
				Bulgaria 407		
				Afghanistan 404		

TABLE 3

Political Instability Profiles of Eighty-Four Countries (1948 – 1965)
(Stability Score Averaged)

1

Netherland	04021
Luxembourg	03012

2

United Kingdom	07112
Ghana	07106
Austria	07057
Denmark	07030
Iceland	07026
West Germany	06087
Finland	06056
China (Taiwan)	06039
Australia	06026
Sweden	06020
Ireland	05031
Saudi Arabia	05018
New Zealand	05015

3

Belgium	10162
Chile	10156
Mexico	10111
Uruguay	10100
Israel	10064
Liberia	10036
Ethiopia	10034
Italy	09192
Libya	09069
Romania	09060
Costa Rica	09058
Afghanistan	09029
Canada	08084
Switzerland	08042
Norway	08034

4

France	13435
Union of So. Africa	13422
Brazil	13209
Morocco	13194
Portugal	13190
Turkey	13189
Poland	13179
Thailand	13152
Jordan	13145
Cyprus	13123
Hungary	13113
Philippines	13105
Czechoslovakia	13100
China (Mainland)	13086
Cambodia	13071
India	12360
Iran	12237
Pakistan	12231
Sudan	12189
U.S.S.R.	12165
Ecuador	12117
Nicaragua	12096
United States	11318
Spain	11284
Dominican Repub.	11195
Ceylon	11152
Japan	11123
Malaya	11108
Yugoslavia	11077
Bulgaria	11071
Albania	11067

5

Argentina	16445
Bolivia	16318
Cuba	16283
Iraq	16274
Colombia	16244
Burma	16213
Venezuela	15429
Syria	15329
Korea	15291
Haiti	15205
Peru	15196
Greece	14236
Guatemala	14234
Lebanon	14212
Egypt	14152
Paraguay	14141
East Germany	14138
Laos	14129
Tunisia	14126
Honduras	14105
Panama	14101
El Salvador	14079

6

Indonesia	18416

Stability ————→ Instability

these scales, and this wealth of data, additional cross-national global profiles and analyses are feasible.

Table 2 is an estimate of global instability combining all the instability events and scaling them.[7] Countries are rated for a seven-year period, and they are assigned to the six-scale groups that appear in these columns on the basis of the most unstable event that took place during 1955–1961. The country rank within the columns is determined by the summed scale values of all events experienced in that country. In this fashion, the intensity of violence as well as frequency of its occurrence is taken into account. New Zealand during these seven years happened to be the most stable nation in the world. No conflict event is reported for this nation. On the other hand, Indonesia and Cuba were the most unstable nations, victims of civil war. The United States, placing itself in the third-scale column, may be judged as quite a stable country during this time period, not the maverick it is in Table 1.

Table 3 captures the instability profiles for a longer, eighteen-year period, 1948–1965.[8] To avoid a highly skewed distribution, instability scores are averaged for three six-year subperiods. As can be seen, only Indonesia remains at scale position 6, indicating that it has experienced civil war during each of the three separate periods. It may also be noticed that the United States is just about in the middle of the violence continuum. Its stability profile has somewhat deteriorated as compared with the previous table. This is the reflection of the more turbulent sixties, especially the explosive racial issue. In the 1956–1960 period, for example, the United States experienced no events that registered higher than position 3 on the six-point scale, but from 1961–1965 twelve percent of this country's events were at scale position 4. This trend of increased violence is also striking with assassinations. Among the sixteen assassinations noted for this country in Table 1, twelve occurred in the 1960s.

Table 4 presents yet another profiling of the eighty-four nations, but this time it is the amount of coerciveness-permissiveness that is depicted; one is tempted to say the amount of democracy or, conversely, the amount of tyranny. Rather than in the assigned individual scores, the countries in this table are simply grouped into six groups, while the entire post–World War II period is taken into account.[9]

The four tables of global aggression patterns are only examples of what we can do with the data. Beyond similar assessments, we try to compare these violence profiles with other characteristics of nations—social, political, economic, or other properties. In this way, we try to ascertain those characteristics of nations which are associated with violence and those that are associated with internal stability. We may also ascertain threshold conditions for political aggression and violence. This endeavor leads us into correlational analysis. For example, we have found the highest likelihood of internal stability occurring in countries that are minimally 90 percent literate; have 65 radios, 120 newspapers, and 20 telephones per thousand people; a diet of 2,525 calories per person per day; a physician for every 1,900 persons; a gross national product of $300 per person per year; and 45 percent of its population living in urban centers.[10] This is a partial ecological image of the average nonviolent nation, so to speak. Below these threshold values, the less industrialized, transitional countries show a marked increase in political violence.

In pursuing correlational analyses, we are guided by theories, and some of our work could be characterized as hypothesis testing. We rely heavily on motivational theories, especially the frustration-aggression construct of social psychology.[11] We accept the fundamental thesis that it is frustration that breeds aggression and hence political violence. We speak of systemic frustration to indicate the relevant social background of frustration. Systemic frustration is broadly conceived as the discrepancy between social goals and aspirations and their satisfactions; and also it is the discrepancy between social expectations of goal achievement, and actual achievement. It is not just indicated in the sense of deprivation that is felt now, but it is also the fear of future deprivation. Furthermore, systemic frustration is given in the sense of uncertainty of social

TABLE 4

Level of Coerciveness

1. Highly Permissive	2. Permissive	3. Mildly Coercive	4. Moderately Coercive	5. Coercive	6. Highly Coercive
Australia	Belgium	Austria	Bolivia	Afghanistan	Albania
Canada	Costa Rica	Brazil	Colombia	Argentina	Bulgaria
Denmark	Finland	Burma	Ecuador	Cuba	China (Mainland)
Netherlands	Iceland	Cambodia	El Salvador	Egypt	China (Taiwan)
Norway	Ireland	France	Ghana	Ethiopia	Czechoslovakia
Sweden	Israel	Greece	Honduras	Haiti	Dominican Republic
Switzerland	Italy	India	Guatemala	Korea	East Germany
United Kingdom	Luxembourg	Japan	Indonesia	Morocco	Hungary
United States	Mexico	Malaya	Iran	Nicaragua	Poland
	New Zealand	Pakistan	Iraq	Paraguay	Romania
	Uruguay	Panama	Jordan	Portugal	U.S.S.R.
	West Germany	Philippines	Laos	Saudi Arabia	Yugoslavia
		Turkey	Lebanon	Spain	
			Libya	Union of So. Africa	
			Peru	Venezuela	
			Syria		
			Sudan		
			Thailand ·		
			Tunisia		

expectations, and finally, it may be the result of conflicts of social aspirations or expectations. With similar motivational hypotheses in mind, we try to identify social situations and processes that may trigger these states of systemic frustration and lead to violence. Let us name a few: the transitional process that jars traditional societies, introducing them to modern aspirations and expectations; wide fluctuations in the social environment; inconsistent policies; institutional incongruence; sudden or rapid deteriorations, and also improvements in economic and societal fortunes.

Such enumeration, however, does not exhaust the possibility of additional, general hypotheses. Even if systemic frustration is present within a country, political stability still may be predicted:

1. If it is a nonparticipant society, lacking relevant strata capable of organizing political action.
2. If it is a participant society in which constructive solutions to frustrating situations are available or anticipated. The effectiveness of government and especially the legitimacy of regimes will be relevant factors.
3. If a sufficiently coercive government is capable of preventing overt acts of hostility against itself. Coerciveness of government, however, must also be interpreted as systemic aggression.
4. And finally, if the aggressive impulse is displaced in aggression against minority groups, and/or against other nations. Also, if individual acts of aggression are sufficiently abundant to provide an outlet.

However, in the relative absence of these qualifying conditions, aggressive behavior in the form of political instability and violence is likely to occur as a consequence of systemic frustration.[12]

It is possible to render several generalizations that stem from our analyses of the cross-national data. First of all, there are definite patterns of violence discernible in our data. It is as if

TABLE 5

Relationship Between Level of Social Frustration and
Degree of Political Stability *

Degree of Political Stability	Index of Social Frustration Ratio of Want Formation to Want Satisfaction		Total
	High Social Frustration	Low Social Frustration	
Unstable	Bolivia Iran Brazil Iraq Bulgaria Italy Ceylon Japan Chile Korea Colombia Mexico Cuba Nicaragua Cyprus Pakistan Dom. Republic Panama Ecuador Paraguay Egypt Peru El Salvador Spain Greece Syria Guatemala Thailand Haiti Turkey India Venezuela Indonesia Yugoslavia 34	Argentina Belgium France Lebanon Morocco Union of So. Africa 6	40
Stable	Philippines Tunisia 2	Australia Norway Austria Portugal Canada Sweden Costa Rica Switzer- Czechoslovakia land Denmark United Finland States West Germany Uruguay Great Britain Iceland Ireland Israel Netherlands New Zealand 20	22
Totals	36	26	62

Chi Square = 30.5, p. = <.001　　　　　　　　　Yule's Q = .9653

* The number of cases in this and the following tables varies with the
available data.

different chemistries of violence were at work in different groups of nations. Not only the intensity and frequency of violence is vastly different among nations, but so is its character. The sort of violence experienced in Western democracies differs from that experienced by the communist bloc or the underdeveloped countries. In modern nations, the United States for example, internal turmoil is largely given by protest events rather than conspiracies or events of internal war.[13] Second, in the broadest sense, the patterns of violence are related to other variables in the environment, the political systems, as well as other social conditions. This much is already implied in the ecological profile of the stable nations.

We found that systemic frustration estimated as a discrepancy (ratio) between the formation of modern aspirations and their achievements has a definite effect on political stability and violence. Formation of modern wants was measured by literacy rates and urbanization, while the achievement of social wants was measured by such indicators as gross national product per capita, distributions of radios, newspapers, telephones, and physicians within the nations.[14] The relationship between this measure of frustration and stability is illustrated in Table 5. The countries in this table are dichotomized according to the aggression profiles shown in Table 2, and the same countries are dichotomized on the other variable, social-frustration-satisfaction.

As can be seen from this table, high frustration is strikingly associated with political instability, and low social frustration or satisfaction is associated with political stability. However, as can be seen, there are also deviant countries registered in the table.

Let us mention some other findings of our cross-national studies:

1. Levels of socioeconomic development or levels of modernity among the nations are curvilinearly related to political instability. Modern countries tend toward stability, transitional developing nations are markedly unstable,

TABLE 6

Frequency of Assassination by Combined Suicide and Homicide Rates

	Low Suicide Low Homicide	High Suicide Low Homicide	Low Suicide High Homicide	High Suicide High Homicide	
High Frequency of Assassinations (3 or more)	Greece (5) Italy (3)	Czechoslovakia (5) France (14)	Burma (5) Colombia (7) Dominican Republic (7) Ecuador (3) Egypt (14) Guatemala (12) India (8) Jordan (6) Mexico (3) Nicaragua (5) Panama (5) Philippines (15)	Brazil (12) Japan (9) United States (16)	
	2	2	12	3	19
Low Frequency of Assassinations (2 or less)	Canada (1) Ireland (0) Netherlands (0) New Zealand (1) Norway (0) Spain (2)	Austria (1) Belgium (1) China (Taiwan) (0) Denmark (0) Iceland (0) Luxembourg (0) Poland (0) Portugal (2) Sweden (0) Switzerland (0) United Kingdom (0) West Germany (2)	Chile (0) Costa Rica (2) Peru (0)	Australia (2) Bulgaria (0) Ceylon (2) Finland (0) Hungary (1) Uruguay (0)	
	6	12	3	6	27
Totals	8	14	15	9	46

Chi Square = 14.59 $p < .01$

and truly undeveloped traditional countries tend to be more stable than countries in the throes of transition.[15]

2. Rapid socioeconomic change usually produces turmoil although the situation may differ for different indicators or measurements of change.[16]

3. International aggression seems quite unrelated to our measures of systemic frustration, although it does seem to relate to internal violence.[17]

4. Suicide rates are positively related to political stability and homicides to political instability.[18] Such a relationship is illustrated in Table 6 in reference to political assassinations.

5. Let us also note that minority-majority tensions, that is, aggression and violence stemming from religious, linguistic, ethnic, or racial issues seem quite unrelated to our aggregate measures of systemic frustration, levels of modernity, or rates of socioeconomic change.[19] As international conflicts, they seem to follow a separate logic.

We may be a little less brief about our findings concerning the coerciveness-permissiveness of political regimes. Let us ask the question, can the use of force, coerciveness, and government repression effectively control civil strife? This is undoubtedly as important a problem within the contemporary setting in the United States as it is for many countries, especially those that are threatened with serious internal disturbances. In a common sense consideration of this question, punishment often is used to stop undesirable conduct. On the other hand, one could also argue that punishment and repression, far from having a pacifying effect, may further anger the recipients and further increase the appetite for aggressive behavior. Table 7 answers this question in terms of cross-national evidence. Tables 2 and 3 were employed in the construction of this table.

In this table, countries are trichotomized into permissive (scale positions 1 and 2), moderate (scale positions 3 and 4), and coercive (scale positions 5 and 6), and the same countries

TABLE 7

Relationship Between Coerciveness and Political Stability

	Permissive	Moderate	Coercive	
Stable	Australia Belgium Canada Costa Rica Denmark Finland Iceland Ireland Israel Italy Luxembourg Mexico Netherlands New Zealand Norway Sweden Switzerland United Kingdom United States Uruguay West Germany	Austria Ceylon Ecuador Ghana Liberia Libya Malaya	Afganistan Albania Bulgaria China (Taiwan) Dominican Republic Ethiopia Nicaragua Romania Saudi Arabia Spain U.S.S.R. Yugoslavia	
	21	7	12	40
Unstable		Bolivia Brazil Burma Cambodia Chile Colombia Cyprus El Salvador France Honduras Greece Guatemala India Indonesia Iran Iraq Japan Jordan Laos Lebanon Pakistan Panama Peru Philippines Sudan Syria Thailand Tunisia Turkey	Argentina China (Mainland) Cuba Czechoslovakia East Germany Egypt Haiti Hungary Korea Morocco Paraguay Poland Portugal Venezuela Union of So. Africa	
	0	29	15	44
Totals	21	36	27	84

TABLE 8

Relationship Between Fluctuation of Coercion and Political Instability

	Low Fluctuation of Coercion	High Fluctuation of Coercion	
Stable	Afganistan Albania Australia Austria Belgium Bulgaria Canada Costa Rica Ethiopia Finland Ghana Iceland Ireland Israel Italy Japan Liberia Libya Luxembourg Malaya Mexico Netherlands New Zealand Norway Saudi Arabia Spain Sweden Switzerland United Kingdom United States U.S.S.R. Uruguay 32	Dominican Republic Ceylon Chile Ecuador Nicaragua Romania West Germany 7	39
Unstable	Cambodia Cyprus East Germany France Iraq Morocco Philippines Portugal Tunisia Union of So. Africa 10	Argentina Bolivia Brazil Colombia Cuba Czechoslovakia Egypt El Salvador Haiti Honduras Hungary India Indonesia Jordan Laos Lebanon Panama Pakistan Paraguay Poland Peru Sudan Syria Thailand Turkey Venezuela 26	36
Totals	42	33	75

are dichotomized into stable and unstable countries. It appears that permissive countries are stable and nonviolent. In fact, all twenty-one permissive countries, without exception, are stable; however, the moment a modicum of coercion sets in, the situation is reversed. Moderate use of force seems to act as a stimulant to internal turmoil, and this is illustrated in the middle column of the table. Of the thirty-six moderately coercive countries, twenty-nine are unstable, while only seven are stable. Furthermore, it would seem that the pacifying effect of coercion takes hold only within extremely coercive regimes. This is illustrated in the last column of the table.[20]

To compare levels of coerciveness with political instability does not tell the whole story. Let us ask another question. What is the effect of inconsistent and arbitrary use of force on political violence? It is well to suppose that the use of excessive force at one point and little or no force at another will give rise to conflicting expectations and uncertainty, while such arbitrariness might also violate expectations of social justice. Such undue fluctuations in the political environment or elsewhere were already postulated as leading to systemic frustration.

We tried to measure the consistency of coerciveness in a cross-national sample by rating countries on a yearly basis for the post–World War II period. There are differences among the countries in their consistency pattern. Table 8 dichotomizes countries into those experiencing low and high fluctuation and into stable and unstable countries. Of forty-two countries that experience low fluctuation of coerciveness, thirty-two are stable, and of thirty-three countries that are high in fluctuation, twenty-six are unstable. Inconsistency of force and coerciveness seems to breed internal turmoil.[21]

If we combine the two variables, level and fluctuation of coerciveness, a very striking patterning emerges. Examining Table 9, one may conclude that all seventy-five countries behave as expected with the exception of seven countries, the four countries in the second and the three countries in the last

TABLE 9

Relationship Between Level and Fluctuation of Coercion and Political Instability

	Permissive	Coercive	Moderate	Permissive	Coercive	Moderate	
Stable	Australia Belgium Canada Costa Rica Finland Iceland Ireland Israel Italy Luxembourg Mexico Netherlands New Zealand Norway Sweden Switzerland United Kingdom United States Uruguay	Afganistan Albania Bulgaria Ethiopia Saudi Arabia Spain U.S.S.R.	Austria Ghana Japan Liberia Libya Malaya	West Germany	Dominican Republic Nicaragua Romania	Ceylon Chile Ecuador	
	19	7	6	1	3	3	39
Unstable		East Germany Morocco Portugal Union of So. Africa	Cambodia Cyprus France Iraq Philippines Tunisia		Argentina Cuba Czechoslovakia Egypt Haiti Hungary Paraguay Poland Venezuela	Bolivia Brazil Colombia El Salvador Honduras India Indonesia Jordan Laos Lebanon Panama Pakistan Peru Sudan Syria Thailand Turkey	
	0	4	6	0	9	17	36
Totals	19	11	12	1	12	20	75

column of the table. The two cells in this table should have remained empty.

In conclusion, we may refer to the socioeconomic characteristics of the stable country presented above and add to this image the political character of either a high level of permissiveness or of coerciveness, coupled with the consistency shown by such a pattern. This type of stable country is the modern, highly developed nation with low rates of socioeconomic change. It tends toward a low level of conflict in its international dealings. Its population is relatively homogeneous, having no strong minorities in its midst. Also, it seems to be a country with a low rate of criminal violence and a high suicide rate. If such a country is modern and permissive and nonetheless tends toward some political aggressiveness, the expressions of violence will have the character of protest rather than conspiracy or internal war. It should be remembered that such a list of traits does not pretend to exhaust the syndrome of traits of political violence. Also, in a broad sweep and in an approximate fashion, it only surveys the global panorama of political violence. It does not claim to penetrate the intricacies of patterns of individual countries, not to mention individual outbursts of political aggression, violence, or revolution.

REFERENCES AND NOTES

1. We are grateful for the support of the National Science Foundation (Grant No. GS-1781) which made possible the cross-national investigation of political violence.
2. A portion of this data collection is on file with the Inter-University Consortium for Political Research, Ann Arbor, Michigan. In due time, all of it will be available.
3. For more detail see Ivo K. Feierabend et al., "Political Violence and Assassination: A Cross-National Analysis," *Assassination and Political Violence*, ed. James F. Kirkham, Sheldon G. Levy, and William Q. Crotty, A Report to the National Commission on the Causes and Prevention of Violence (Washington, D. C.: U. S. Government Printing Office, 1969).

4. For factor analyses of conflict data, see Rudolf J. Rummell, "Dimensions of Conflict Behavior Within and Between Nations," *General Systems Yearbook,* 1963; and Raymond Tanter, "Dimensions of Conflict Behavior Within and Between Nations, 1958–1960," *Journal of Conflict Resolution,* March 1966.

5. For more detail see Ivo K. Feierabend and Rosalind L. Feierabend, *Cross-National Data Bank of Political Instability Events (Code Index)* (San Diego, Calif.: Public Affairs Research Institute, San Diego State College, 1965); and Betty A. Nesvold, "A Scalogram Analysis of Political Violence," *Comparative Political Studies,* July 1960.

6. Jennifer G. Walton, "Correlates of Coerciveness and Permissiveness of National Political Systems: A Cross-National Study" (Master's thesis, San Diego, Calif.: San Diego State College, 1965); Ivo K. Feierabend et al., "Level of Development and International Behavior," *Foreign Policy and the Developing Nation,* ed. Richard Butwele (Lexington: University of Kentucky Press, 1969); and Rosalind L. Feierabend et al., "Inter-Group Conflict: A Cross-National Analysis" (Paper delivered at the Annual Meeting of the American Political Science Association, September 1969).

7. For more detail see Ivo K. Feierabend and Rosalind L. Feierabend, "Aggressive Behavior Within Polities, 1948–1962: A Cross-National Study," *Journal of Conflict Resolution,* September 1966.

8. Ivo K. Feierabend, Rosalind L. Feierabend, and Betty Nesvold, "Social Change and Political Violence: Cross-National Patterns," *Violence in America: Historical and Comparative Perspectives,* ed. Hugh David Graham and Ted Robert Gurr, A Report to the National Commission on the Causes and Prevention of Violence (Washington, D. C.: U. S. Government Printing Office, 1969).

9. I. K. Feierabend and R. L. Feierabend, "The Relationship of Systemic Frustration, Political Coercion, International Tension and Political Instability" (Paper delivered at the Annual Meeting of the American Psychological Association, September 1966); also in "Systemic Conditions of Political Violence," *Readings in Political Violence,* ed. Ivo K. Feierabend, Rosalind L. Feierabend, and Ted Robert Gurr (Englewood Cliffs, N. J.: Prentice-Hall, 1970, to be published).

10. See Feierabend and Feierabend, "Aggressive Behavior Within Polities."

11. For a comprehensive statement of the theory, see John Dollard et al., *Frustration and Aggression* (New Haven, Conn.: Yale University Press, 1939); Leonard Berkowitz, *Aggression: A Social Psychological Analysis* (New York: McGraw Hill, 1962); and Ted Robert Gurr, *Why Men Rebel* (Princeton, N. J.: Princeton University Press, 1970).

12. See Feierabend et al., "Social Change and Political Violence.

13. Ted Robert Gurr, "A Comparative Study of Civil Strife," *Violence in America,* ed. Graham and Gurr.

14. Feierabend and Feierabend, "Aggressive Behavior Within Polities."
15. *Ibid.;* see also Feierabend et al., "Social Change and Political Violence."
16. Feierabend and Feierabend, "Aggressive Behavior Within Polities"; see also Wallace W. Conroe, "A Cross-National Analysis of the Impact of Modernization upon Political Stability" (Master's thesis, San Diego, Calif.: San Diego State College, 1965).
17. Feierabend et al., "Level of Development and International Behavior."
18. Feierabend et al., "Political Violence and Assassination."
19. Feierabend et al., "Inter-Group Conflict."
20. Feierabend and Feierabend, "The Relationship of Systemic Frustration."
21. Betty A. Nesvold et al., "Regime Coerciveness and Civil Disorder" (Paper delivered at the Annual Meeting of the American Political Science Association, September 1969).

Simulations in the Consolidation and Utilization of Knowledge about International Relations*

HAROLD GUETZKOW

Northwestern University
Evanston, Illinois

Editor's note: Dr. Guetzkow opened his talk with an observation that it was Moratorium Day in Washington, D. C., stating that previous speakers had used analogies and theatrics, "and I wonder if you would allow me to symbolize my relationship to this day." With that Dr. Guetzkow removed his jacket, walked to left stage, and hung it on one of the wings of the eagle atop the flag pole that was holding the American flag.

At the end of Dr. Guetzkow's address, the first questioner inquired as to the symbolic hanging of his coat on the flag, in particular, was it an intentional act of disrespect to our nation's flag?

"No, it wasn't. It was just the opposite. The reason I'm here today rather than at the Moratorium is that I think we're on the right track and I'm awfully proud that I can hang up my coat and roll up my sleeves beside the flag of my country," Dr. Guetzkow stated firmly.

"Good for you, sir," responded the questioner.

Subsequent to the meeting, Dr. Guetzkow was sent a typewritten copy of his address to edit for this proceeding. In reviewing his remarks, Dr. Guetzkow came to the conclusion that the document that best spoke to the published title of his paper was the following paper (also by Guetzkow), from which much of the material presented came. Whereas the talk at the ASC meeting was a summary of the state of the art of man-computer simulations of international processes and a brief look at the future, the attached document (complete with references) provides an in-depth analysis of the problems involved in developing such simulations.

---

*This paper was originally prepared for the Simulated International Processes Project conducted within the International Relations Program at Northwestern University. It also appeared in Dean G. Pruitt and Richard C. Snyder (Editors), *Theory and Research on the Causes of War,* Prentice-Hall, 1969. Copyright 1967 by Northwestern University. Reproduced with the permission of the copyright holder and by courtesy of Prentice-Hall.

119

In the last decade and a half, important gains have been made in the number and quality of research studies in the field of international relations, evidenced by such empirical pieces as those assembled by J. David Singer (1967) and by the essays constituting this book (Pruitt and Synder, 1969). If the trend continues, there will be an increasing need for ordering and integrating the knowledge generated in such studies—and an opportunity for the application of the findings, in ongoing decisions by policy-makers of the world. During this same period of time, a capability to simulate complex international processes was created by the development of a variety of simulation formats (Guetzkow, 1966a) and by the invention of simulation languages (Naylor, et al., 1966, Chapter 7).

This essay explores the potentiality of using simulations as devices for ordering theories and for integrating empirical findings. Buttressed by verbal deliberations on the one hand and by mathematical formulations on the other, can simulations implement the ability of decision-influencers to use such theories and findings in international policy-making? At the end of this presentation, a proposal is developed to illustrate one way in which work with simulations might be organized for the consolidation and utilization of knowledge about international relations.

Simulations as a Format for Theory

Over the past centuries it has been customary to express political, economic, social, and psychological theory in words—in the vernacular of the times, after the demise of Latin as the *lingua franca*. With the development of mathematics, scholars possessed a vehicle by which they might express their loose verbal formulations with more explicitness, separating their assumptions from the derivations which follow as consequences of their analyses (Alker, 1965). But both of these formats for the development of theories have shortcomings. The serial nature of verbal exposition, with one thought following another on the written page, imposes serious limitations. Likewise, the intractability of many mathematical systems, once non-linear formulations are involved, seriously handicaps the investigators. Building upon both verbal and mathematical expositions, contemporary scholars are exploring the usefulness of simulations as devices for handling complex materials, both theoretical and empirical (Dawson, 1962; Naylor, *et al.*, 1966; Evans, *et al.*, 1967, Chapter 1, pp. 1–15). In the social sciences, a simulation may be conceived as "an operating representation in reduced and/or simplified form of relations among social units [i.e., entities] by means of symbolic and/or replicate component parts" (Guetzkow, 1959, p. 184).

Simulations in international relations attempt to represent the on-going international system or components thereof, such as world alliances, international organizations, regional trade processes, etc. Clark Abt and Morton Gorden (1968) and their associates have represented such processes as perception, homeostasis, and bargaining, through a digital computer simulation called TEMPER, a *T*echnological, *E*conomic, *M*ilitary, *P*olitical *E*valuation *R*outine. Harold Guetzkow and his associates (Guetzkow, Alger, Brody, Noel, and Snyder, 1963) have developed man-machine constructions (sometimes called "games") in which the decision-making processes are handled by human participants serving as surrogates for the international actors, whilst national processes are formulated through some thirty equations, the computation of which serves to represent the capabilities and consequences of the decision-making. Lincoln P. Bloomfield and his associates (Bloomfield and Whaley, 1965), following earlier developments by Hans Speier and others at the RAND Corporation (Goldhamer and Speier, 1959), used the "political exercise" in which crisis gaming among area experts is monitored by a "control team" which serves to umpire moves developed in response to an on-going scenario. This "all-manual" (as distinguished from the "all-computer") format is now used intensively at high levels within some parts of the United States government (Giffin, 1965). Because the control team operates principally in terms of intuitive verbal theory as it directs the progress of the game, allowing and disallowing particular international behaviors and imposing consequences on the various countries' teams, this simulation style in the long run may not prove as useful a format for the consolidation of knowledge as will man-computer and all-computer simulations. Further, it seems that, as the state of the computer arts becomes more adequate and our knowledge about international affairs grows more explicit and is grounded on a better data-base, man-machine constructions will be replaced by all-computer simulations. Already this has occurred, for example, in the development of formulations about legislatures, which moved from James S. Coleman's all-manual game (Coleman, 1963) to the all-computer simulation of voting in the Eighty-eighth Congress by Cleo H. Cherryholmes (1966) and Michael J. Shapiro (1966).

Consolidating Knowledge About International Relations Through Simulations

As we move into the latter third of the Twentieth Century, it seems feasible to catalyze the consolidation of our knowledge about international affairs through the use of simulations. Verbal efforts to present holistic integrations of extant knowledge are found in the textbooks of international relations. Yet, their contents are theoretically vague and their data bases are largely anecdotal as Denis G. Sullivan points out (Sullivan, 1963; especially his "Conclusions," pp. 305–313). Mathematical formulations, such as those by Lewis F. Richardson (1960), are more partial in scope, even though they are explicit in structure and systematic in their grounding in data. When an attempt is made to be comprehensive, as occurred in the work of Rudolph J. Rummel (1966), the mathematical theory tends to be at a metalevel, more statistically theoretical than substantively explicit.

How can simulations be used as vehicles for accumulating and integrating our knowledge, both in its theoretical and its empirical aspects, building upon the contributions of those who work in ordinary language as well as of those who use the language of mathematics?

Simulations may serve in three ways as formats through which intellectuals may consolidate and use knowledge about international relations: (1) Simulations may be used as techniques for increasing the coherence within and among models, enabling scholars to assess gaps and closures in our theories; (2) Simulations may be used as constructions in terms of which empirical research may be organized, so that the validity of our assertions may be appraised; (3) Simulations may be used by members of the decision-making community in the development of policy, both as devices for making systematic critiques, through "box-scoring" its failures and successes, and as formats for the exploration of alternative plans for action.

(1) Simulations in the Differentiation and Amalgamation of Theories in International Relations

Simulations of the international system are frameworks into which both verbal and mathematical formulations may be incorporated, therein combining something of the rigor of a mathematical model, which an all-computer simulation is (Guetzkow, 1965), with the comprehensiveness of a verbal inventory (Snyder and Robinson, 1961 [sic]). Quincy Wright (1955) noted years ago in his *Study of International Relations* that our knowledge of international affairs develops in fragments. What is examined piecemeal, however, must eventually be reassembled, especially if the knowledge is to be used in policy work, where problems come as wholes. Once differentiated, our findings must be amalgamated.

The appearance of "handbooks" in the social sciences, consisting of chapters which attempt integrative summaries of bodies of literature, such as the one developed by Herbert C. Kelman (1965) on *International Behavior*, dramatizes how knowledge tends to be developed segmentally, composing "islands of theory" (Guetzkow, 1950, pp. 426, 435, 438, *et passim*). The contributors to a handbook single out a componential process within international affairs, such as "Bargaining and Negotiation" (Sawyer and Guetzkow, 1965), foci which are sometimes differentiated in much detail elsewhere, as in this case in the exciting verbal treatments by Fred Charles Iklé in *How Nations Negotiate* (1964) and by Arthur Lall in *Modern International Negotiation* (1966). In parallel, a body of quasimathematical work may develop, as in this same instance is found in the Theory of Games (Shubik, 1964). Within a simulation, aspects of both streams of theory may then be consolidated as a nodule or a modular—as each subroutine of a simulation is sometimes designated—as was done by Otomar Bartos in developing a negotiating routine for international trade in which he used the rubrics of J. F. Nash's mathematically formulated "solution" (Sherman, 1963).

The "reader," exemplified in the influential compilation of *International Politics and Foreign Policy* (Rosenau, 1961), uses juxtaposition as a tool for the integration of knowledge. But, a more closely articulated and systematic integration of components is now possible through the use of simulation. As Paul Smoker and John MacRae demonstrate in their reconstruction of the Inter-Nation Simulation to explore the Vietnam situation, it is possible to take an already existing model of international affairs and incorporate additional and revised components within the existing framework (MacRae and Smoker, 1967, see Appendix, pp. 11–23). For example, in this Canadian/English simulation of the Vietnam situation, the collaborators were able to use Smoker's earlier work (Smoker, 1965) with the Richardson model in a rigorous development of polarization as dependent upon both trade and defense (MacRae and Smoker, 1967, pp. 16–17, *cf.*, "The Computer Model" columns) in defining "National Security"—an important feature heretofore absent from the Inter-Nation Simulation.

Simulations, especially those of the all-computer variety, demand a clarity that is unusual in theory building (Guetzkow, 1965, pp. 25–39) in the specification of the entities involved, in the exact involvement of variables used to describe the entities, and in the explicit formulation of the relations among both entities and variables. Once these components of theory have been assembled into a simulation, gaps within the framework become more readily apparent. One reason Walter C. Clemens (1968) elucidated the shortcomings of TEMPER with ease is found in its high level of explicitness (Guetzkow, 1966a). As more and more effort is put into amalgamating part-theories, there will be an increasing need for a standard language within which to construct each such "island of theory," so that they may be readily incorporated into larger, more encompassing constructions.

Despite the difficulties involved, as one of the central architects of TEMPER knowingly testifies (Gorden, 1967), with improvements in simulation languages (Naylor, *et al.*, 1966) it will be possible to articulate one modular with another more easily, if they are all built originally in a common computer language. Then there may be a division of labor among scholars, in which each may work on his components with a thoroughness worthy of his specialization. Then, when his "islands of theory" are placed within a simulation, the researcher may become aware of the broader issues that are relevant to his area of focus.

The complexities of theory, which are impossibly cumbersome when the ideas are formulated verbally in textbooks (Scott, 1967) and intractable when the ideas are structured as models (Orcutt, 1964, pp. 190–191), may become more amenable when simulations are used to organize the division of labor more coherently among the scholars working with international affairs, providing for a differentiation of effort as well as for an amalgamation of findings.

(2) Simulations as Vehicles in the Validation of Theories in International Relations

Simulations of the international system are devices through which empirical findings may be organized, so that the validity of their theoretical contents may be assessed. With the coming increase in the number of "data-making" studies (Singer, 1965, pp. 68–70) of the "real world," as reference materials are sometimes designated, there is need for consolidation of these empirical findings, as well as integration of our theories. Theory of all kinds—be it verbal, verbal-mathematical, or simulation—needs to be validated. As Charles F. Hermann has pointed out, it is important for many purposes to determine the degree of correspondence between the simulation model and the reference system (Hermann, C. F., 1967, p. 220), whether one is interested in the variables and parameters of the model (*ibid.*, p. 222), in the similarity or dissimilarity of the array of events produced in both simulation and the world (*ibid.*, pp. 222–23), or in determining whether the same hypotheses hold in both model and reference systems (*ibid.*, pp. 223–24). When policy work is based on explicitly formulated theory, it is possible to judge the adequacy of policy alternatives more adequately if the extent of its validation is known.

Man-machine and all-computer simulations, especially, provide a systematic, somewhat rigorous technique for the appraisal of the validity of theory. Richard W. Chadwick (1966) has shown how correspondences between hypotheses embodied as assumptions about the functioning of national political systems may be checked out against empirical data gathered from the reference system of years centering on 1955. For example, he found that, although the likelihood of a decision-maker to continue in office is assumed in the simulation to be a function both of the latitude the decision-maker has in constructing his policies and the extent to which his supporters are satisfied with the consequences of his policies, the hypothesis holds in the international reference system of 1955 only with respect to the latter (Chadwick, 1966, p. 11).

Guetzkow (1967) was able to examine over twenty studies in which one or more operations in simulations of international processes were each paralleled by an empirical finding. These ranged from correspondences in the form of anecdotes about events [such as the fact that a conference, called by Lord Grey of England in the prelude to World War I and never assembled, proved to be the vehicle by which the issue was resolved by the participants in the Hermanns' adaptation of the Inter-Nation Simulation representing European developments in the summer of 1914 (Hermann and Hermann, 1967, pp. 407–8)] to correspondences between relationships among variables [such as the linear function between national consumption standards and the satisfaction of the groups which validate the office-holders (Elder and Pendley, 1966, p 31)]. In his summary of particular comparisons of simulation outputs with data from the reference system, Guetzkow found there was "Some" or "Much" congruence in about two-thirds of the fifty-five instances available from the twenty-three studies, providing a kind of "box-score" on the simulations. These findings, taken in conjunction with achievements being realized through simulation in other parts of the social sciences (Guetzkow, 1962a), foreshadow the fruitfulness of cumulating findings on the validity of theory as it has been integrated within an operating simulation model.

Simulations are not only apt vehicles for making studies of the systematic, rigorous validations of theory. When used for such purposes, they also heuristically spin off ideas for revising theory about international processes. For example, in the man-computer format Dina A. Zinnes demonstrated an inadvertant error in the construction of the Inter-Nation Simulation: by omitting the buffer role of embassies between the home nation's foreign office and the foreign offices of other nations, a "small groups" effect was elicited, in which a cycle of even more hostility leading to less communication leading further to even more hostility exacerbated itself (Zinnes, 1966, pp. 496, 498–99). This effect was not found in the relations among the European capitals in the summer of 1914. Now it is possible to reconstruct the simulation so as to avoid this so-called "autistic hostility" phenomenon (Newcomb, 1947). Another example of the way in which validation study of simulation theory aids in its revision is found in Robert E. Pendley and Charles D. Elder's re-definition of the meaning of "officeholding" in the programmed components of the Inter-Nation Simulation (INS) in terms of contemporary verbal theory and data on the stability of regimes and governments. After comparing ways in which the simulation and the reference system behave, they conclude that "INS theory is a fairly good predictor of stability, but that it is the stability of the political system rather than stability of particular officeholders that the theory explains" (Pendley and Elder, 1966, p. 25).

Thus, simulations are useful devices through which efforts in the validation of their theoretical soundness may be organized when outputs of simulations are compared with corresponding characterizations in the reference system. Further, in the very process of making the comparisons one has a heuristic tool through which verbal and mathematical speculation can be grounded empirically to provide a base for the revision of simulation theory. Unless simulation theory is validated, it would seem unwise to use it for "decision-making" in the policy-making community.

(3) Simulations in the Utilization of Knowledge for Policy-Making in International Affairs

Were a body of consolidated knowledge about international affairs available, it would seem that simulations might aid in the utilization of that knowledge—for monitoring on-going events as well as for the construction of "alternative futures." The myriad of actors within the international system—be they members of planning units in foreign ministries, entrepreneurs in businesses operating overseas, or officials within governmental and non-governmental international organizations—base their decisions for actions upon their assumptions of the ways in which this system functions, combined with their assessments of its present state. Simulations may increase the adequacy with which knowledge about international affairs is utilized in the conduct of foreign affairs, by providing explicit theories as to how the system operates, as well as by providing a continuously up-dated data-base. A somewhat comprehensive list of "Some Areas of Knowledge Needed for Undergirding Peace Strategies," presented elsewhere (Guetzkow, 1962b, pp. 90–91), runs the gamut of such topics as "initiative and coordination within national security decision machinery" and "international communications." Simulations, geared to the policy problems confronting the public and private decision-makers of the world, can serve in two ways as aids in the utilization of this knowledge: (a) in being a framework within which the antecedents and consequences of on-going policy decisions can be examined, and (b) in being a way of considering alternative futures of the international system, either as contingencies or as ends whose paths-to-achievement may be plotted.

(a) *"Box-Scoring" Policy Decisions.* In the hurly-burly of organizational life, there is seldom time for explicit analyses of the effectiveness of "hits" and "misses." Seldom does the decision-maker systematically sort out the way the antecendents in his decision situations eventuate in their consequences. Yet, today there are increasingly adequate techniques of both verbal and mathematical varieties available, which help in structuring knowledge so that it may be used more effectively in decision processes. For example, the verbal analyses involved in program-planning and budgeting procedures now being urged throughout government (Chartrand and Brezina, 1967) are becoming more and more sophisticated in their specification of the means-ends chains involved in cost-benefit analyses (Grosse, 1967). With the mathematization of "optimizing techniques" within operations research (Carr and Howe, 1964), miniature theories are being constructed about the assessment of the influence of factors upon outcomes. These verbal and mathematical sources of explication are making it feasible to construct on-going simulations of policy processes of decision-making, as illustrated in extant all-computer models of budgetary processes of municipalities (Crecine, 1965). In the arena of international relations, it also would seem possible to use simulations as vehicles for the explication of decision-making processes, thereby "box-scoring" policy-making.

Suppose a policy-planning group in a country's disarmament and arms control bureau were interested in making an analysis of the relations among antecedents and consequences of their policy decisions with respect to the nation's postures in a multilateral "standing group" operating in Geneva. It might then erect a simulation of the international system and run it parallel with the policy deliberations. For example, it might combine a negotiation exercise (Bonham, 1967) within the context of a man-computer simulation of international processes (Smoker, 1967), tailored to fit conditions of the moment. Were there disagreement within the staff, two or more alternative simulations could be explored, changing the parametric weighting given to particular variables, and even substituting one nodule for another, allowing them to "compete" as to adequacy. Through such a double-nested simulation, it would be possible to examine developments at two levels—in terms of (1) the on-going conference situation in Geneva, and (2) the changes in the overall international political scene itself. In examining the immediate situation, they could simulate the action of the committee of principals within the foreign policy machinery of the government itself, along with responses of opposite numbers, of allies, and of non-aligned nations—once policy proposals were activated in the international arena. In examining the context of the work of the multilateral group, one would simulate the arms race within regions as well as globally, including the impact of the failure to achieve a non-proliferation treaty as well as the consequences of already agreed-upon treaties, such as the test-ban.

One operation of the simulation might be molded to be strictly congruent with on-going policies. Then the developments—both antecedents (in structure and process) and consequencies (in outcomes and feedbacks)— could be "box-scored," as the events of the international system unfolded week-by-week, month-by-month. In fact, were alternative simulations operating simultaneously a few weeks or months ahead of the decisions of this committee of principals, their outputs might be used for policy development within the arms control and disarmament agency, were they satisfied with the extent of the validity of these simulation results.

Such a "box-scoring" procedure would demand an explication of the theories (which now are often being used without clear formulation by the policy-makers of the assumptions involved), so that an appropriate simulation (with its competing variations) might be adapted from extant models in forms useful for policy problem-solving. Further, in requiring the tallying of successes and failures, the procedure would eventuate in a careful validation of the simulation. The modulars composing the antecedent processes as postulated by the policy-makers would be assessed as to whether they yield their predicted consequences in the "real world." Note that these two steps are the same two procedures involved in the consolidation of knowledge by basic researchers concerned with international affairs, as outlined in the previous sections of this essay: (1) the amalgamation of verbal and mathematical theory in a simulation's constructions, and (2) its validation through empirical confrontations.

To use simulation as an instrument for policy development would be to have a powerful tool by which the ever increasing richness of theory and data might be brought to bear upon decision-making in international affairs by the policy-influencers of the world throughout the remainder of this century. But such "box-scoring" procedures would not only be of aid to the policy-makers; the applied work would have important feedbacks into research. It would provide a vehicle by which the thinking of outstanding political leaders might be fed back into the academic community, so that its work might benefit from the creativity of the policy community. Further, on-going comparisons between expectations and realities, made week-by-week over the years, would highlight congruences and incongruences between the simulation model—in its many variations—and central aspects of the reference system.

(b) *Exploring Alternative Policy Futures.* Simulations are an important heuristic in their potential for representing alternative, future states of affairs which to date have been non-existent (Boguslaw, 1965). As knowledge is consolidated through simulation, enough confidence may be gained eventually to use such constructions for the systematic exploration of alternative futures (de Jouvenel, 1963, 1965). Although, certainly, theory should be data-based, simulations must not be "data-bound" (Guetzkow, 1966b, pp. 189–91).

Efforts to use simulations for the exploration of possible futures are in their infancy. An example in miniature of such pioneering in an all-computer format is found in the U.S. Department of State's analysis by computer of the consequences of various voting arrangements within the United Nations. The simulation was applied to "178 key votes that took place in the General Assembly between 1954 and 1961," the weighting being based on population and contributions to the UN budget. Richard N. Gardner reports that while the weightings "would have somewhat reduced the number of resolutions passed over U.S. opposition, they would have reduced much more the number of resolutions supported by the United States and passed over Communist opposition. The same conclusion was reached in projecting these formulas to 1970, having regard to further increases in membership" (Gardner, 1965, p. 238). Using a man-computer format, Richard A. Brody experimented in the summer of 1960 with the effects of the proliferation of nuclear capabilities upon alliances (Brody, 1963). Working from an inventory of some thirty-six verbal propositions in the literature about the "Nth country problem," Brody designed a variation of the Inter-Nation Simulation so that consequences of an antecedent spread of nuclear weapons technology among nations might be studied. Brody found a "step-level change in the 'cold war system'" after the spread of nuclear capability: Threats external to each bloc were re-reduced, and threats internal to each bloc were increased, accompanied by a decrease in bloc cohesiveness; the original bipolarity of the system was fragmented (Brody, 1963, p. 745). A final example, employing the manual technique of the political-military exercise, is found in the recent exploration by Bloomfield and his colleagues of the "possible future employment of United Nations military forces under conditions of increasing disarmament" in the context of the U.S. proposals of April 18, 1962, on General and Complete Disarmament (GCD) (Bloomfield and Whaley, 1965). After investigating four hypothetical crises—indirect aggression and subversion in Southeast Asia, a colonial-racial civil war in a newly independent African nation, a classic small-power war in the Near East, and a Castro-type revolution in Latin America—Bloomfield draws a set of policy inferences, including the notion that "disarmament planning might well consider whether an appropriate plateau for the GCD process can be found somewhere" (*ibid*, p. 864).

The use of simulation for sketching alternatives may prove in the long run to be a useful implement in the reconstruction of our international system, should we ever devote enough resources toward the generation and consolidation of knowledge so as to give us the validity to make such constructions viable. In the creation of unprecedented alternative futures (Huntington, *et al.*, 1965), can we manage with verbal speculation alone—or with mathematical formulations only? Perhaps, as we gain experience in amalgamating modulars which have been grounded in empirical findings, we will, someday, have the ability to construct futures which are more than visionary.

These are the goals, then: to develop simulation theory, in the context of verbal speculation and mathematical constructions about the structures and processes involved in international affairs; to apply a variety of criteria in the validation of such theory, depending upon the purposes for which it is intended; to use for decision-making the knowledge which has been consolidated for purposes of policy development, both in terms of short run "box-scoring" and in the long run for the creation of alternative futures. If such is the potential, the query becomes, "How can we accelerate our rate of accomplishment in achieving these goals?"

Accelerating the Consolidation and Utilization of Knowledge about International Relations through Standing Colloquia

Let this essay conclude with a proposal for acceleration in the study of international relations through the establishment of *colloquia* centering on simulations, so that there may be a continuous dialogue between theory builders, empirical researchers, and policy developers. Perhaps the time is now appropriate for a more integrative, long range effort than is possible alone through doctoral dissertations, textbooks, collections of juxtaposed readings, handbooks of summary pieces, substantive inventories developed for special occasions, and *ad hoc* conferences and committee reports. Given the pace of the explosion of knowledge within the international relations area (Platig, 1966, pp. 3–11), which the foregoing efforts are yielding, it seems imperative that a technique of potential efficacy be explored to hasten a tighter, more cumulative articulation of this knowledge.

There now are some fifteen to twenty sites throughout the world at which simulations of international affairs are being conducted. These operations vary widely in their magnitude and quality, as well as in their styles. Only a few of these will nurture their activities into full-fledged centers worthy of adequate, continuous support.

One or more such units probably will operate within a university setting, with its efforts undergirded by the relevant disciplines and its output available to all throughout the world. Such university-related centers would provide training in simulation for scholars and professionals interested in foreign affairs. With the recent emergence of the autonomous research organization, it is difficult to believe that such "think-tanks" (Reeves, 1967)—be they of a "for profit" or a "non-profit" variety—will not give serious attention to simulation work. Perhaps some of the international companies will develop their considerable knowledge, obtained in commercial operations overseas, through special corporate staffs concerned with the simulation of the international system in which they operate, with some focus on the role of the non-governmental organizations. In the decades ahead, at least a dozen or so units concerned with simulation may be established within agencies of different governments in the world. In developing their foreign policies toward each other, there may emerge a common core of data and theories, even though each foreign office—just like each international company—will probably develop for its own exclusive use a simulation base of secret contents. Little wonder, then, that the international organizations—most appropriately perhaps the United Nations Institute for Training and Research—will need to lead the development of simulation models, so that all countries, regardless of their resources in the social sciences, may have access to a universal model for the exploration of the antecedents and political consequences of their policies. Because of the exemplary work the United Nations Secretariat has done on its statistical services in decades past, a universal data-base for simulation work is already well advanced.

Within the last five years there has been a considerable growth in bodies of empirical data which have been and are being generated through elections, interview surveys, and the like (Bisco, 1966). Perhaps now is the time to develop somewhat analogous *standing colloquia,* so that those developing theory—be it verbal or mathematical in style—may consolidate their work. Were one such colloquium staffed with a secretariat, perhaps it could provide a means by which theorists could relate with more intimacy and rigor to the data-gatherers and data-makers. In addition, such a colloquium would provide a forum in which policy-influencers might have their formulations dialogued. It may turn out that just as a number of data consortia are developing throughout the world, there may be more than one colloquium—different modes of simulation and different purposes may demand different kinds of colloquia for varying styles of collaboration. For example, already it seems that those interested in the uses of simulation for education and training are centering their efforts in ways different from those using simulations as vehicles for theory construction and validation (Coleman, Boocock, and Schild, 1966).

How might a colloquium implement collaboration among four to five simulation centers located in different parts of the world? Through a working director—who would probably need to be a young, flexible theorist of some distinction—the secretariat of the colloquium might develop an integrated model of the international system, as was suggested above. In the process of constructing the model over a period of some five to ten years, periodic sessions with theorists—regardless of the mode in which they work—would be convened, so that a consolidation of fruitful and adequately verified components of theory might be incorporated into the colloquium's simulation. The staff of the colloquium would compare the assumptions underlying extant simulations and design experiments for assessing the importance of the differences. To obviate the need to operate its own simulation in its early years, it might invite three or four simulations already in operation—perhaps on sub-contract—to address the same inquiry, so that systematic comparison among the various alternative models might be made, in the style pioneered by Hayward R. Alker, Jr. and Ronald D. Brunner (1967).

Without attempting to operate its own data consortium, how might the staff of the colloquium manage to ground its model in the findings from such research? It might review the empirical literature to assess the extent to which components of its model are being validated. It might then develop recommendations, in the mode of inventories, as to where further empirical work was needed, coordinating the execution of such research so that there would be close matching between simulation and reference materials. With an ever increasing volume of research being generated through Programs of Area Study as well as in the more traditional Centers of International Studies (Snyder, 1968), the staff of the colloquium might usefully provide a liaison service, so that the developing simulations throughout the world would be more closely articulated with outpourings in empirical research, both of a qualitative and quantitative variety. In fact, just as a member of the colloquium's secretariat might be designated to work with the verbal theory of the more speculative scholars in order to incorporate their ideas into the simulation, so might a special staff member be assigned the task of developing the theory which emerges from empirical studies into a form that could be phrased as modular sub-routines for use in the colloquium's simulation. In fact, it is easy to understand how the colloquium might pay special attention to achievements in simulation in other parts of the social sciences, too, so that full advantage could be taken of developments in the field of artificial intelligence (for the development of foreign policy decision-making models) and in the field of organizational simulation (for the development of inter-nation system models), for example.

In all the activities of the colloquium, policy-related professionals would be involved intimately so that their decision-makers—be such located in foreign offices, in international corporations, or in international organizations—might develop operations in tandem with those evolving in the colloquium. Were some consensus to emerge through the good offices of the colloquium, various simulation groups throughout the two hemispheres might exchange modules, as well as use each other's data-bases—on perhaps multilateral as well as bilateral bases. Which centers will effect a collaboration so that their competitive efforts will become cooperative, too—as in the fashion of the SSRC/Brookings Economic Quarterly Model of the United States (Duesenberry, et al., 1965)? It is exciting to imagine the officers of inter-parliamentary unions of the regions of the world contracting with colloquia for systematic exploration of some items on their agenda, so that their deliberations might be grounded in the fruits of social sciences, as such are represented in the consolidation of knowledge about international affairs through simulations.

Collaboration among simulation centers will be accelerated mightily with the coming of world-wide computer systems, which might be shared by centers comprising a core group which has proven its ability to work together in an integrative way. Through the leadership of the Western Behavioral Sciences Institute, John Raser and his overseas colleagues—from Japan, Mexico, and Norway—already are gaining experience in the practicality of cooperation in cross-cultural research involving man-computer simulations (Solomon, Crow, and Raser, 1965). Should the work of the colloquium be successful, such centers would operate in a common computer language, making possible the integration of their work. Should the efforts of the colloquium be achieving its goals, the same group of centers would be sharing data-bases using common variables, all commensurable with each other. Eventually the colloquium's function would be merely that of coordinating the operation of a communication-by-satellite system of validated simulations. Then, the policy-makers of the world might all join freely such an international net, building our world futures through cooperative endeavor.

As Hans J. Morgenthau asserts, "What is decisive for the success or failure of a theory is the contribution it makes to our knowledge and understanding of phenomena which are worth knowing and understanding. It is by its results that a theory must be judged . . . " (Morganthau, 1967, from "Preface to the Fourth Edition). Will the use of simulation as a vehicle in the consolidation and utilization of knowledge in international relations enable us to develop theory, the results of which will give us a better world than the one we've lived in for the last quarter century, whose policy roots have been dominated by the babel of theory posed in ordinary tongues?

Summary

What is simulation's potential for the consolidation and utilization of knowledge about international affairs? Although all-computer and man-computer simulations, as well as all-manual political exercises, may be employed as devices for training participants, simulations may also be used as a way of positing theory and deriving its consequences. Simulations may be used as a tool for the integration of widely used verbal theory, as well as for theory which is developed in mathematical language. Simulations encourage explicitness in formulation and permit the coherent amalagamation of subtheories into interactive, holistic constructions of great complexity. Further, using simulation as the format for formulating theory enables systematic and rigorous work to be achieved in the validation of its interrelated parts, feeding back heuristically into reformulations of aspects of the model which are less than congruent with the empirical materials. Finally, data-grounded simulations may aid in the development of policy, both in terms of its evaluation as well as in terms of its creation. By monitoring on-going events with simulations operated in parallel, "box-scores" can be derived for appraising the adequacy of unfolding policies. By using these same simulations as devices for the examination of alternative futures, modification in short term policies can be made and long-run forecasts can be mounted.

In conclusion, a proposal is made for acceleration of the consolidation and utilization of knowledge about international affairs through the establishment of standing colloquia. Analogous to the growing consortia being developed throughout the world for amassing and retrieving political data, it is proposed that special standing colloquia be developed among scholarly and governmental centers, so that competing simulations, along with their verbal theories and mathematical formulations, might be used integratively as ways of coordinating the development and use of knowledge about international relations.

REFERENCES

Abt, Clark, and Morton Gorden. "Report on Project TEMPER." In Dean G. Pruitt and Richard C. Snyder (Editors), *Theory and Research on the Causes of War*. Englewood Cliffs, New Jersey: Prentice-Hall, Inc., 1969.

Alker, Hayward R., Jr. *Mathematics and Politics*. New York: The Macmillan Company, 1965.

Alker, Hayward R., Jr. and Ronald D. Brunner. "Simulating International Conflict: A Comparison of Three Approaches." Mimeo. New Haven, Connecticut: Yale University, July, 1967.

Bisco, Ralph L. "Social Science Data Archives: A Review of Developments." *American Political Science Review*, 40, 1 (March, 1966), 93–109.

Bloomfield, Lincoln P., and Barton Whaley. "The Political-Military Exercise: A Progress Report." *Orbis*, 8, 4 (Winter, 1965), 854–870.

Boguslaw, Robert. *The New Utopians: A Study of System Design and Social Change*. Englewood Cliffs, New Jersey: Prentice-Hall, Inc., 1965.

Bonham, G. Matthew. "Aspects of the Validity of Two Simulations of Phenomena in International Relations." Ph. D. Dissertation. Cambridge, Massachusetts: Department of Political Science, Massachusetts Institute of Technology, 1967.

Brody, Richard A. "Some Systemic Effects of the Spread of Nuclear-weapons Technology: A Study through Simulation of a Multi-nuclear Future." *The Journal of Conflict Resolution*, 7, 4 (December, 1963), 663–753.

Carr, Charles R. and Charles W. Howe. *Quantitative Decision Procedures in Management and Economics*. New York: McGraw-Hill Book Company, 1964.

Chadwick, Richard W. "An Empirical Test of Five Assumptions in an Inter-Nation Simulation, about National Political Systems." Evanston, Illinois: Simulated International Processes project, Northwestern University, August, 1966.

Chartrand, Robert L., and Dennis W. Brezina. "The Planning-Programming-Budgeting System: An Annotated Bibliography." Washington, D. C.: The Library of Congress Legislative Reference Service, April 11, 1967.

Cherryholmes, Cleo H. "The House of Representatives and Foreign Affairs: A Computer Simulation of Roll Call Voting." Ph. D. Dissertation. Evanston, Illinois: Department of Political Science, Northwestern University, August, 1966.

Clemens, Walter C. "TEMPER and International Relations Theory: A Propositional Inventory." In William D. Coplin (Editor), *Simulation Models of the Decision-Maker's Environment*. Chicago: Markham Publishing Co., 1968. Presented at Wayne State University Symposium, Detroit, Michigan, May 10–13, 1967.

Coleman, James S. "The Great Game of Legislature." *The Johns Hopkins Magazine*, (October, 1963), 17–20.

Coleman, James S., Sarane S. Boocock, and E. O. Schild (Editors). *In Defense of Games, American Behavioral Scientist*, Part I, 10 (October, 1966); *Simulation Games and Learning Behavior. American Behavioral Scientist*, Part II, 10 (November, 1966).

Crecine, John P. "A Computer Simulation Model of Municipal Resource Allocation." Ph. D. Dissertation. Pittsburgh, Pennsylvania: Carnegie Institute of Technology, 1965.

Dawson, Richard D. "Simulation in the Social Sciences." In Harold Guetzkow (Editor), *Simulation in the Social Sciences: Readings*. Englewood Cliffs, New Jersey: Prentice-Hall, Inc., 1962, 1–15.

De Jouvenel, Bertrand (Editor). *Futuribles: Studies in Conjecture*. Geneva, Switzerland: Droz, 1963 and 1965.

Duesenberry, J. S., G. Fromm, L. R. Klein, and E. Kuh (Editors). *The Brookings Quarterly Economic Model of the United States*. Chicago: Rand, McNally & Co., 1965.

Elder, Charles D., and Robert E. Pendley. "An Analysis of Consumption Standards and Validation Satisfactions in the Inter-Nation Simulation in Terms of Contemporary Economic Theory and Data." Evanston, Illinois: Department of Political Science, Northwestern University, November, 1966.

Evans, George W., II, Graham F. Wallace, and Georgia L. Sutherland. *Simulation Using Digital Computers*. Englewood Cliffs, New Jersey: Prentice-Hall, Inc., 1967.

Gardner, Richard N. "United Nations Procedures and Power Realities: The International Apportionment Problem." *Proceedings of the American Society of International Law*, 59th Meeting (April, 1965), 232–245.

Giffin, Sidney F. *The Crisis Game: Simulating International Conflict.* Garden City, New York: Doubleday & Company, Inc., 1965.

Goldhamer, Herbert, and Hans Speier. "Some Observations on Political Gaming." *World Politics*, 12, 1 (October, 1959), 71–83.

Gorden, Morton. "Burdens for the Designer of a Computer Simulation of International Relations: The Case of TEMPER." In Davis B. Bobrow (Editor), *Computers and The Policy-Making Community Application to International Relations.* Englewood Cliffs, New Jersey: Prentice-Hall, Inc., 1968. Presented at the Institute held at Lawrence Radiation Laboratory, University of California, Livermore, California, on April 4–15, 1966.

Grosse, Robert N. "The Application of Analytic Tools to Government Policy: The Formulation of Health Policy." In William D. Coplin (Editor), *Simulation Models of the Decision-Maker's Environment.* Chicago: Markham Publishing Co., 1968. Presented at Wayne State University Symposium, Detroit, Michigan, May 10–13, 1967.

Guetzkow, Harold. "Long Range Research in International Relations." *The American Perspective*, 4, 4 (Fall, 1950), 421–440.

Guetzkow, Harold. "A Use of Simulation in the Study of Inter-Nation Relations." *Behavioral Science*, 4 (1959), 183–191.

Guetzkow, Harold (Editor). *Simulation in the Social Sciences: Readings.* Englewood Cliffs, New Jersey: Prentice-Hall, Inc., 1962a.

Guetzkow, Harold. "Undergirding Peace Strategies through Research in Social Science." In Gerhard S. Nielsen (Editor), *Psychology and International Affairs: Can We Contribute?* Proceedings of the XIV International Congress of Applied Psychology, Volume I. Copenhagen, Denmark: Munksgaard, 1962b, 88–96.

Guetzkow, Harold. "Some Uses of Mathematics in Simulations of International Relations." In John M. Claunch (Editor), *Mathematical Applications in Political Science.* Dallas, Texas: The Arnold Foundation, Southern Methodist University, 1965, 21–40.

Guetzkow, Harold. "Simulation in International Relations." In *Proceedings of the IBM Scientific Computing Symposium on Simulation Models and Gaming.* York, Pennsylvania: Maple Press, 1966a, 249–278.

Guetzkow, Harold. "Transcending Data-Bound Methods in the Study of Politics." In James C. Charlesworth (Editor), Monograph 6, *A Design for Political Science: Scope, Objectives, and Methods.* Philadelphia: The American Academy of Political and Social Science, December, 1966b, 185–191.

Guetzkow, Harold. "Some Correspondences Between Simulations and 'Realities' in International Relations." Evanston, Illinois: Northwestern University, 1967. In Morton Kaplan (Editor), *New Approaches to International Relations.* New York: St. Martin's Press, 1967.

Guetzkow, Harold, Chadwick F. Alger, Richard A. Brody, Robert C.

Noel, and Richard C. Snyder. *Simulation in International Relations: Developments for Research and Teaching.* Englewood Cliffs, New Jersey: Prentice-Hall, Inc., *1963.*

Hermann, Charles F. "Validation Problems in Games and Simulations with Special Reference to Models of International Politics." *Behavioral Science,* 12, 3 (May, *1967*), 216–231.

Hermann, Charles F., and Margaret G. Hermann. "An Attempt to Simulate the Outbreak of World War I." *American Political Science Review,* 61, 2 (June, *1967*), 400–416.

Huntington, Samuel P., Ithiel De Sola Pool, Eugene Rostow, and Albert O. Hirschman. "The International System." In *Working Papers* of the *Commission on the Year 2000* of *The American Academy of Arts and Sciences,* Volume V. Boston: The American Academy of Arts and Sciences, *circa 1965.*

Iklé, Fred Charles. *How Nations Negotiate.* New York: Harper and Row, *1966.*

Kelman, Herbert C. (Editor). *International Behavior: A Social-Psychological Analysis.* New York: Holt, Rinehart and Winston, *1965.*

Lall, Arthur. *Modern International Negotiation: Principles and Practice.* New York: Columbia University Press, *1966.*

MacRae, John, and Paul Smoker. "A Vietnam Simulation: A Report on the Canadian/English Joint Project." *Journal of Peace Research,* 1 (*1967*), 1–25.

Morgenthau, Hans J. *Politics Among Nations: The Struggle for Power and Peace.* New York: Alfred A. Knopf, *1967* (Fourth Edition).

Naylor, Thomas H., Joseph L. Balintfy,. Donald S. Burdick, and Kong Chu. "Introduction to Computer Simulation." In their *Computer Simulation Techniques.* New York: John Wiley and Sons, Inc., *1966,* 1–22.

Newcomb, Theodore M. "Autistic Hostility and Social Reality." *Human Relations,* 1 (*1947*), 69–86.

Orcutt, Guy H. "Simulation of Economic Systems: Model Description and Solutions." *Proceedings of the Business and Economic Statistics Section, American Statistical Association, 1964,* 186–193.

Pendley, Robert E., and Charles D. Elder. "An Analysis of Office-Holding in the Inter-Nation Simulation in Terms of Contemporary Political Theory and Data on the Stability of Regimes and Governments." Evanston, Illinois: Department of Political Science, Northwestern University, November, *1966.*

Platig, Raymond E. *International Relations Research: Problems of Evaluation and Advancement.* New York: Carnegie Endowment for International Peace, *1966.*

Pruitt, Dean G., and Richard C. Snyder (Editors). *Theory and Research on the Causes of War.* Englewood Cliffs, New Jersey: Prentice-Hall, Inc., *1969.*

Reeves, Frank. "U. S. Think-Tanks: The New Centers for Research and Thought, and Their Growing Impact on American Life." A series of five articles in *The New York Times,* June 12–16, *1967.*

Richardson, Lewis F. *Arms and Insecurity*. London: Stevens and Sons, Ltd., *1960*.

Rosenau, James (Editor). *International Politics and Foreign Policy: A Reader in Research and Theory*. New York: The Free Press, *1961*.

Rummel, Rudolph J. "A Social Field Theory of Foreign Conflict Behavior." Prepared for Cracow Conference, 1965. *Peace Research Society (International) Papers, 4 (1966)*, 131–150.

Sawyer, Jack, and Harold Guetzkow. "Bargaining and Negotiation in International Relations." In Herbert C. Kelman (Editor), *International Behavior: A Social-Psychological Analysis*. New York: Holt, Rinehart and Winston, *1965*.

Scott, Andrew M. *The Functioning of the International Political System*. New York: The Macmillan Company, *1967*.

Shapiro, Michael J. "The House and the Federal Role: A Computer Simulation of Roll Call Voting." Ph. D. Dissertation. Evanston, Illinois: Department of Political Science, Northwestern University, August, *1966*.

Sherman, Allen William. "The Social Psychology of Bilateral Negotiations." M. A. Thesis. Evanston, Illinois: Department of Sociology, Northwestern University, *1963*.

Shubik, Martin (Editor). *Game Theory and Related Approaches to Social Behavior*. New York: John Wiley and Sons, Inc., *1964*.

Singer, J. David. "Data-Making in International Relations." *Behavioral Science*, 10, 1 (January, *1965*), 68–80.

Singer, J. David (Editor). *Quantitative International Politics: Insights and Evidence in World Politics. International Yearbook of Political Behavior Research*, Volume VI. New York: The Free Press (Macmillan), *1967*.

Smoker, Paul. "Trade, Defense, and the Richardson Theory of Arms Races: A Seven Nation Study." *Journal of Peace Research*, II (*1965*), 161–176.

Smoker, Paul. "International Processes Simulation." Evanston, Illinois: Simulated International Processes project, Northwestern University, *1967*.

Snyder, Richard C. "Education and World Affairs Report." New York: *1968*.

Snyder, Richard C., and James A. Robinson. "The Interrelations of Decision Theory and Research and the Problem of War and Peace." *National and International Decision-Making*. New York: Institute for International Order, *1961* (*sic*), 16–25.

Solomon, Lawrence N., Wayman J. Crow, and John R. Raser. "A Proposal: Cross-Cultural Simulation Research in International Decision-Making." La Jolla, California: Western Behavioral Sciences Institute, June, *1965*.

Sullivan, Denis G. "Towards An Inventory of Major Propositions Contained in Contemporary Textbooks in International Relations." Ph. D. Dissertation. Evanston, Illinois: Department of Political Science, Northwestern University, *1963*.

Wright, Quincy. *The Study of International Relations*. New York: Apple-ton-Century-Crofts, *1955*.

Zinnes, Dina A. "A Comparison of Hostile Behavior of Decision-Makers in Simulate and Historical Data." *World Politics*, 18, 3 (April, *1966*), 474–502.

Modeling the Dynamics of Warfare*

JOHN VOEVODSKY

Cybernetica Research Corporation
Stanford, California

The Vietnam War is demonstrated to be an orderly, mathematically lawful, behavioral event.

During the last 100 years,† the United States has fought four major wars to conclusion: the Civil War, World War I, World War II, and the Korean War. For the past ten years, we have been engaged in a fifth and not yet concluded war, the war in Vietnam, which has occupied our minds, our troops, and our resources longer than any other war in our history.

And yet, despite its record duration, the Vietnam War appears to be progressing, as of this writing, in the same orderly manner as our four previous wars. An inquiry into the repetitive behavioral patterns of nations at war, particularly of the United States, our allies, and our enemies during the last 100 years, reveals that we and the enemy are acting today in the same way as we have acted in the past. Because of this orderliness of our behavior, it now appears that we may be at

*This article is based on research performed while a Research Associate, Department of Psychology, at Stanford University and while a consultant to the Office of the Chief of Naval Operations, USN.

†This cybernetic analysis is based on a purely descriptive examination of the data—the vital statistics—of modern nations at war, particularly the United States, our allies, and our enemies during the last 100 years. No attempt is made to explain the processes which result in the behavioral orderliness. The data of all five wars are seen to fit very closely the same, simple, mathematical laws.

a point in the Vietnam War where either a settlement is possible or another major escalation is indicated.

This study is based on an examination of the phenomena—the vital statistics—of modern armed conflict by means of cybernetic analysis. It is purely of an exploratory nature (it should be emphasized), and no pretense is made that it is possible at present to explain fully and in detail all the factors which result in the orderly progress of the Vietnam War.

All such endeavors, though, however bravely undertaken and whatever their results may be, have a theoretical origin. This research is no exception. In fact, it has two origins: one in the quantitative behavioral concepts of the psychologist S. S. Stevens,[1] and the other in the cybernetic concepts of the mathematician Norbert Wiener.[2] In essence, Stevens shows that quantification of behavior is readily achieved by the assignment of numerals to distinguishable behavioral events in the careers of living systems. These behavioral events become the system variables, which are time variant. The system variables, in addition, appear to have the characteristics inherent in linear second-order feedback-control systems of the type first conceived by Wiener. Furthermore, the work on the quantitative nature of warfare performed by L. F. Richardson[3] and F. W. Lanchester[4] supports these general observations.

The Vital Statistics of War

The quantitative behavioral data which best describe modern warfare fall into three categories: battle strength, battle casualties, and battle deaths. By coincidence, these are the vital statistics of war, because nations habitually count their troops, assess their attrition, and record the results of combat for current and historical uses. From the point of view of the analyst, though, these particular items of data have a value in addition to their ubiquity. They have an advantage over other war statistics because they appear to be remarkably stable and accurate, since in most cases they have stood the scrutiny of countless researchers over long periods of time.

It should be further emphasized that only official government sources are used for the statistics in this analysis, with two exceptions. French and German battle deaths and casualties during World War I were taken from Winston S. Churchill's compilation of official records.[5] Union and Confederate statistics for the Civil War were taken from Thomas L. Livermore's compilation of official records.[6]

The basic vital statistics, battle strength, battle casualties, and battle deaths, unless carefully defined, may mean different things to different analysts. In this analysis, the numbers used for all wars represent only army personnel, officers and enlisted men, reported at the specified instant of time that is under consideration. This applies whether the troops are Union, Confederate, French, German, British, or American. In the case of the Vietnam War, however, numbers of total Department of Defense forces, which includes the United States Army, U.S. Navy, Marine Corps, and the Coast Guard, are used separately and in addition to the numbers used for the army personnel.

For the United States Army, battle strength is the total number of officers and enlisted men at any time, t, deployed in the battle zone. For the Vietnam War, the battle zone is considered to be South Vietnam, and the number of army personnel in South Vietnam at any instant is considered to be the army battle strength.[7] This does not include army personnel who are off shore or are in any other location such as Thailand.

Army battle strength for the Korean War is the total number of army personnel on the Korean Peninsula at any instant;[8] for World War II, it is the total number stationed outside the continental limits of the United States at any instant of time;[9] for World War I it is the total number in France, at any instant.[10] Similarly, British army battle strength is the total number of British army personnel in France at any instant of time during World War I.[11] Comparative statistics for German army battle strength during World War I were not available in suitable form.

For the Civil War, the Union army battle strength is the total number of personnel on the Union rolls at any instant, and the Confederate army battle strength is the total number of personnel on the Confederate returns at any instant.[12] Of all the war statistics included in this analysis, the Civil War strength data show the widest fluctuations and are considered the least reliable of all the data.

Army battle casualties for the Vietnam War,[13] the Korean War,[14] and World War II[15] are the accumulated totals from the beginning of the particular war up to any time, t, of all army personnel killed in action, dead as the result of wounds or injuries received in action, wounded or injured in action, missing in action, captured by the opposing forces, or taken into custody as internees by the authorities of a neutral country. The term *in action* characterizes a casualty status in which an individual suffered death or injury as a direct result of enemy action, either while engaged in a battle, going to it, or returning from it. Excluded from United States Army battle casualties are injuries or deaths that resulted from exposure to the elements or from diseases.

Army battle deaths for the Vietnam War, the Korean War, and World War II are the accumulated totals from the beginning of the wars up to any time, t, of army personnel who were killed in action, died as a result of injuries or wounds received in action, or declared dead while missing in action.

For the United States Army in World War I, the time variants in the battle casualties are not known. The time variants in battle deaths are known. Total U.S. battle casualties at the end of World War I include dead, wounded, missing and prisoners.[16] Similarly, mutually caused British versus German,[17] and French vesus German,[18] battle casualties include dead, wounded, missing, and prisoners. Only the American Civil War battle casualties, which included dead and wounded, exclude missing and prisoners because the data was unavailable.[19] The interested auditors of this paper should consult the original sources cited for more detailed definitions of battle strength, battle casualties, and battle deaths.

The British-German and French-German World War I and American Civil War vital statistics should be considered as approximations. Differences exist in the data for each war which must be considered by the analyst as measurement error. The size of the error, unfortunately, is not known at this time. Also, when the analyst compares the errors between wars, he should assume that part of the errors are due to differences in accounting procedures. The errors that might occur in the United States data for the Vietnam War, the Korean War, and World War II, however, can be considered to be the smallest, since statistics for the three wars were compiled by the same government, are close together in time, and major changes in accounting procedures do not appear to have been made. No detailed studies have been made of the exact accounting methods employed by the other governments because of the exploratory nature of this research. The data have been taken more or less on faith from official sources, except where noted. The reader should be assured, however, that when conclusions are drawn, he will be alerted to the possible error in the base statistics so that he may discount the conclusions to the degree he chooses.

Method of Analysis

A mere compilation in tabular form of these three items of data, arrayed over time, reveals very little about the progressive nature of the statistics for a particular war, the relationships that exist between opposing forces in a particular war, or the relationships that exist among the statistics of different wars. Yet it is an identification of these significant relationships that is being sought in this analysis through a graphic and mathematical manipulation of the three sets of vital statistics. Thus, here are identified and separated out for examination the relationships between battle casualties and battle deaths, between battle strength and battle casualties, between opposing forces (the effect of their coupled statistics), and between battle strength and time. Other by-products, such as the effectiveness of weapons systems, can also be identified.

To accomplish this purpose of identifying significant relationships, the standard scientific method of analysis is followed. The published statistics were gathered and put into the form dictated by the theories of Stevens and Wiener. For example, one important feature of the dictated form is to record accumulated totals over time. Any two sets of these data, thus compiled, define coordinate points. Semilog paper is used to plot the relationship of the statistics to time, and log-log paper is used to plot the relationship of one vital statistic to another. This is done because semilog and log-log paper best illustrate the respective exponential and power relationships that were found to exist.

The connection of one data point to another on the graph paper, of course, results in two types of lines. The exponential functions produce curves and straight lines. The power functions produce straight lines. In presenting these data graphically a suitable mean line has been drawn through the data points by inspection. Due to the exploratory nature of the research, it is considered unnecessary to employ more rigorous methods of curve fitting.

Thus, it must be said that the basic method, or scheme of analysis, is not materially different from that followed in any other responsible scientific investigation. What is different here are the items chosen for analysis, the uniqueness of their arrangement, and the results of their manipulation.

Battle Deaths and Battle Casualties

Identification of the mathematical relationship between battle deaths and battle casualties is the first of the four equations presented here to demonstrate the orderly progress of the Vietnam War. The relationship is shown in Fig. 1.

This relationship between battle deaths and battle casualties can be described mathematically from an inspection of the plotted curves by a power function

$$D = \gamma C^\delta,$$

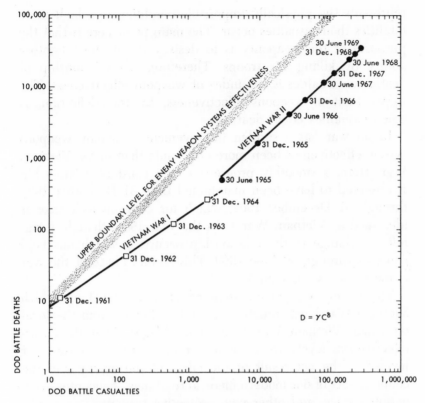

Figure 1. U.S. Department of Defense battle deaths plotted vs. U.S. Department of Defense battle casualties for the Vietnam War.

where D is the battle deaths at any time, t; C is the battle casualties at the same time, and γ and δ are constants, which as a by-product define the net effectiveness of the enemy's weapons system over the effectiveness of all countermeasures designed to protect troops. The symbols γ and δ define a family of curves, or levels, between the battle deaths and battle casualties for each war. This formulation permits the analyst to view a coalition of nations as one weapon system.

Quite automatically, the formulation also establishes the upper boundary of enemy weapons system effectiveness. In Fig. 1 this maximum effectiveness boundary represents points where, at a given time, all battle casualties are also battle deaths. Hence, any data point which falls above this boundary

represents the physically impossible condition in which more
fatalities than casualties occur. The main point here is that the
purposes of the weaponry is to destroy the enemy's fighting
ability by killing his troops. Therefore, the relationship of
deaths to casualties is one index of weapons effectiveness. The
upper limit of weapons effectiveness, by this definition, is
when casualties equal deaths.

In no war has a sudden improvement in enemy weapons
system effectiveness been more noticeable than in the Vietnam
War. Here, a smoothly progressive and constant relationship
is observed to have been maintained from 31 December 1961
through 31 December 1964, which for convenience's sake is
identified as Vietnam War I. In the year 1965, though, a significant change in the relationship occurred, which has held
constant through 30 June 1969. This second phase of the war
is identified as Vietnam War II.

The enemy weapons system effectiveness level on which
Vietnam War I was fought is entirely different from the level
on which Vietnam War II is being fought. That these two
effectiveness levels are under other major United States war
levels[20] is the net result of the effect of the enemy and the
countereffect of our modern medical treatment, helicopter evac-
uation service, and other new protective systems.

These are modern times, though, and this particular enemy
theoretically has access to an even more sophisticated weapon
system than he is now employing. It thus appears possible that
the Vietnam War could suddenly escalate to levels experienced
during the Korean War and World War II and become Asian
War I merely through the introduction of tanks, air power,
missiles, and/or Chinese troops. An escalation in enemy
weapons system effectiveness might also occur simultaneously
through the employment of Chinese- and Soviet-directed tac-
tics and strategies.

Battle Strength and Battle Casualties

Identification of the mathematical relationship between bat-

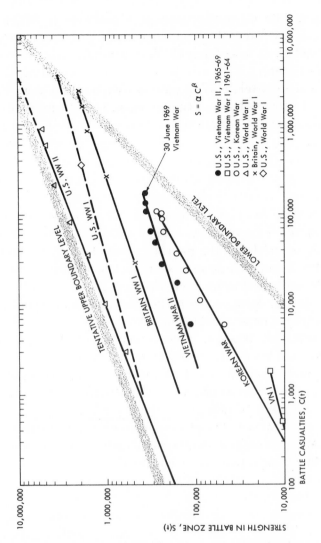

Figure 2. U.S. Army battle strength plotted vs. U.S. Army battle casualties for the major U.S. wars.

tle strength and battle casualties is the second of the four equations presented to demonstrate the orderly progress of the Vietnam War. This relationship is shown in Fig. 2 by a graphic representation of a summary of United States Army statistics for the Vietnam War, the Korean War, World War II, World

War I, and British participation in World War I. Statistics for the Civil War are not included, because the strength figures as a function of time for both sides are known to be of questionable accuracy.

Once again a relationship pattern that is common to all wars analyzed is immediately discernible from an inspection of the plotted curves. This pattern, too, can be described by a power function

$$S = \alpha C^\beta,$$

where S is the total army strength at any time, t; C is the army battle casualties at the same time; α and β are constants, which in combination define the intensity of the fighting in the battle zone. The symbol α also represents the theoretical initial battle zone strength at the moment the first battle casualty is sustained. In this sense, α is a battle-preparedness coefficient and β is the replacement coefficient.

The equation, however, represents other conditions. It states that the number of army troops in a battle zone at a given instant is determined by the battle casualties. It also states the converse. In other words, it implies that each new casualty causes the influx of new troops by a predictable amount and, conversely, that new troops produce additional casualties. This is evident, because if a simple mathematical manipulation (the logarithmic derivative) is taken, then

$$\frac{dS}{S} = \beta \frac{dC}{C}$$

results. From Fig. 2, β is seen to be less than 1, where β varies very roughly from 0.57 for the Korean War, 0.38 for World War II, 0.37 for the British experience in World War I, and 0.36 for Vietnam War I and II. If β were zero, then battle strength would be a constant, α, equal to the initial fighting strength. Thus β is, then, the replacement coefficient, where the strength, when doubled in the battle zone, causes the casualties to go

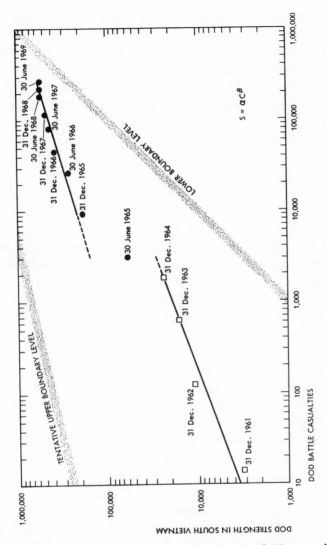

Figure 3. U.S. Department of Defense battle strength in South Vietnam plotted vs. U.S. Department of Defense battle casualties.

up roughly by nine times for all wars considered, except for the Korean War, where they went up roughly by four times.

While it is acknowledged that consideration of five data points, in this case five wars, is not necessarily proof of the existence of a phenomenon, an examination of the relation-

ships between wars suggest that two important conclusions can
be drawn.

First, there are limits in strength buildups and casualties
a nation will sustain, beyond which it either accepts defeat,
changes its leadership, or acquires new allies. This idea is
graphically illustrated in Figs. 2 and 3 for the Vietnam War
alone, by a lower boundary level, which defines the points
where battle casualties and battle strengths are equal.

This line, in effect, represents a boundary to the right of
which a nation cannot seem to pass and still sustain its own war
effort. For example, Great Britain at the end of World War I
suffered roughly two million battle casualties with a total
strength in France at the end of the war of two million soldiers.
Since the population of Great Britain at the time was 60 million, this represents 3.33 percent of her 1918 population. It is
revealing to note that 3.33 percent of the United States population (110 million during World War I) is 3.67 million combat troops, or casualties, which is the point where the United
States experience in World War I intersects the lower boundary
when it is extended as shown by the dashed lines in Fig. 3.

Approximately fifty-five percent of the U.S. Army battle
strength for Korea and for the Vietnam War II are combat
troops. If army combat strength is plotted versus army battle
casualties for Korea and for the Vietnam War, then one finds that
both lie close to the lower boundary level. Furthermore, since
the U.S. Marine Corps has all combat troops and no support
troops it would be expected from the above that the Vietnam
War II would be over when Marine Corps battle strength equal
Marine Corps battle casualties. This has occurred as of this
writing in the Vietnam War II. Finally, as a percentage of
their population, the North Vietnamese have suffered more
than the U.S. Thus, if they cannot obtain new allies (i.e.,
China), they are under greater military pressure per capita to
settle the war than the U.S., provided at least a casualty ratio
of unity is assumed.

Additionally, the estimated absolute ceiling on the number
of men physically fit for active war service for the United

States during World War II was between 15 and 16 million,[21] which again is the intercept of the extension of the United States World War II with the lower boundary level. This point represents 11.4 percent of the United States population of 131 million in 1940.

Finally in World War I, Russia mobilized 15.5 million men. If it is assumed that they could deploy the same percentage of men mobilized as the United States did in World War I, which was 52.7 percent, then theoretically, they could suffer 8.1 million casualties. They actually suffered 7.9 million casualties before their government collapsed. The Russian data is obtained from Nicholas Golovine.[22] Thus, the first conclusion is that a nation cannot pass the lower boundary level and still sustain (on its own) its own war effort. New allies must be introduced or the war settled. As of this writing, the Vietnam War II is at this level.

The second conclusion that can be drawn from an examination of the relationship of battle strength to battle casualties over five wars is that there appears to be an upper boundary level, or limit on the degree of mobilization that a nation's citizens will consent to as they prepare for and participate in a major war. This upper level becomes a sloping line when it is represented on the graph, which in this instance is drawn backward from the point where all potential soldiers could become casualties. The angle of the line is drawn according to a slope that is the average for all wars analyzed. This average slope is $\beta_{ave} = 0.38$.

If one assumes that, as during World War II, 11.4 percent of the United States population represents the maximum number of soldiers that the United States could prepare for combat, then the present 200 million population would produce a potential reservoir of 22.8 million men for the Vietnam War. The data show, however, that a nation does not mobilize all its potential fighting men at once. It characteristically mobilizes gradually as casualties are incurred. Therefore, this gradual mobilization, mathematically represented by $\beta_{ave} = 0.38$, appears to be a behavioral characteristic of warring nations—to

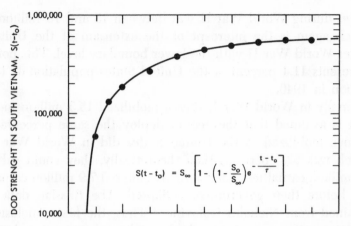

Figure 4a. U.S. Department of Defense strength in South Vietnam plotted from June 1965 to June 1969, where 600,000 is estimated strength of the ultimate forces engaged.

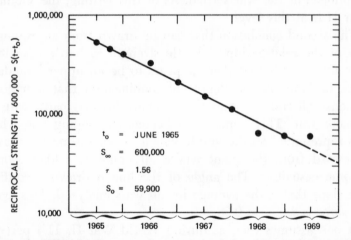

Figure 4b. Difference between the strength of the ultimate Department of Defense forces engaged, 600,000, and the actual Department of Defense strength engaged in South Vietnam at a particular instant plotted vs. time from June 1965 to June 1969.

maintain a balance between the maintenance of combat-eligible men in their normal productive activities in the society and the complete mobilization and commitment to battle of these same men in an effort to protect the nation's way of life.

Finally, when the strength to casualty relationship is applied to the Vietnam War, as illustrated in Fig. 4, it may be clearly seen that a jump in activity occurred in 1965. This was the point at which the United States escalated its strength, expressed mathematically by changing α to a higher level of effort, in coupled response to the change in enemy weapon system effectiveness. For the past three and one-half years the relationship of strength to casualties has not changed materially.

Relationship Between Opposing Forces

The mathematical relationship between strength to strength, casualties to casualties, and deaths to deaths for opposing armies for a particular war is the third of the four equations presented to demonstrate the orderly progress of the Vietnam War. This relationship has been shown for the French versus German armies, and for the British versus the German armies during World War I, and for the Union and Confederate armies during the Civil War.[23] Analyses for the other wars were not made, because data on enemy forces in the Vietnam Wars, and Korean War, and World War II were either not available or were not in suitable form.

Here, too, a discernible relationship can be deduced from the resulting curves, which can be described by a power function

$$Y = jX^k,$$

where X and Y are identical statistics at the same instant of time for opposing forces. The coupling coefficients are j and k. In all cases studied, however, k is found to be almost equal to 1. In fact, k varies between 0.95 and 1.04. Thus, by setting k equal to 1, the coupling relationship assumes the simpler form of

$$\frac{dY}{dX} = j.$$

This equation states that if one side changes its war variables, a similar change occurs on the other side. Lanchester has defined j as the exchange ratio, i.e., the ratio between those combatants lost on one side to those combatants lost on the other. Also, an increase in troops on one side results in an increase in troops on the other. This ratio also is intuitively expected because when two armies come together in combat, firing begins almost simultaneously from both sides. When the combat ends, the firing ends simultaneously on both sides. If a large battle occurs, both sides suffer large losses at the same time. This is true regardless of whether the battle is classified as a success, a failure, a defeat, a rout, or a victory.

Historically, the Germans have been accused of dividing their casualty statistics in half for political purposes. This may or may not be the case. What is important is that the casualty data for both sides have essentially the same shape when plotted. The Civil War also shows this expected characteristic of similarity in shape, and even in magnitude for the casualty statistics. Thus the most important point to be realized here is that if the analyst is interested in when a war begins and when it might end, as indicated by a leveling of hostilities (measured by strengths, casualties, and deaths), he can determine this from the casualty data of only one of the two combatants. True, the other side might have a higher or lower strength ratio, or casualty ratio, or kill ratio, but the leveling of hostilities occurs simultaneously and in like manner on both sides. The reader should be cautioned, however, that this conclusion is based on observation made of only two wars and within these two wars on only six relationships. They are: Union and Confederate strength, Union and Confederate casualties, Union and Confederate deaths, French and German casualties, British and German casualties, and British and German deaths. Thus, on this basis one may conclude that opposing warring nations have similar behavioral patterns over time during a war even though the ratios between statistics may be different.

As this conclusion applies to the Vietnam War, one can say: If the coupling constants do not change, then the leveling of hostilities (as measured by the vital statistics of warfare) is clearly discernible from the United States statistics alone. In other words, if wars are fought on the basis of attrition, and end when one or both sides cannot sustain further casualties, then the measure of this attrition in the system can be seen solely by either sides statistics alone.

Battle Strength and Time

Identification of the mathematical relationship between army battle strength and time is the last of the four equations presented to demonstrate the orderly progress of warfare. Since battle deaths are related to battle casualties and in turn are related to battle strength, the relationship between casualties and between deaths and time can be established by means of algebraic manipulations once the mathematical relationship between battle strength and time is known.

If the behavior of warring nations can be characterized by linear second-order feedback-control systems equations of the type first conceived by Wiener and supported by the work of Richardson, Lanchester, and others,[24, 25] then the solutions are exponential in nature.

The general solution for a second-order system is

$$S = A + Be^{\lambda_1 t} + Ce^{\lambda_2 t},$$

where A, B, C, λ_1, and λ_2 are characteristic constants of the system. For the wars studied it is found that the first exponential term quickly disappears while the strength is less than ten percent of the ultimate forces. The remaining ninety percent of the ultimate fighting force is characterized by only one time constant. Thus, if the analyst is concerned only with the last ninety percent of a war, first-order differential equations appear to describe accurately the time-variant nature of the vital statistics. Second-order equations appear to be needed only when the beginnings of wars are to be analyzed. Since the Vietnam War is found to be in its terminal stages, the first ten percent of wars have not been analyzed.

To develop these ideas, one considers first the case of Viet-

nam War II, shown in Fig. 4a and Fig. 4b. In this case, S denotes the total Department of Defense strength in South Vietnam at any time, t. The variation of battle strength, S, with
time is shown in Fig. 4a. It is seen that if the conditions which
have been acting in a particular manner over the past four
years continue in an unchanged manner, the battle strength, S,
approaches an upper limit, say S_∞, the ultimate number of
forces that are to be engaged. By extrapolation in Fig. 4a, one
finds that S_∞, to a good approximation, is 600,000 Department
of Defense personnel. To obtain a simple analytical representation for the function S, one finds, as shown in Fig. 4b, that
log (S_∞ - S) varies linearly with time, i.e., the curve log
(S_∞ - S) versus t is a straight line. If -1/τ denotes the slope of
this line, and if S_0 denotes S at some initial time, t_0, the equation for the line is

$$\log \left[\frac{S_\infty - S(t - t_0)}{S_\infty - S_0} \right] = - \frac{t - t_0}{\tau}$$

or, equivalently,

$$\frac{S(t - t_0)}{S_\infty} = 1 - \left(1 - \frac{S_0}{S_\infty} \right) e^{-(t - t_0/\tau)}.$$

Generally, for the wars analyzed here, the initial strength,
S_0, is much less than the final strength, S_∞, at least by a factor
of ten. It is therefore, reasonable to assume that the ratio of
initial strength to final strength is much less than one and the
above expression may be expressed in the simpler form of

$$\frac{S(t - t_0)}{S_\infty} = 1 - e^{-(t - t_0/\tau)}.$$

The constant, τ, which has the dimensions of time and is
referred to as the time constant, characterizes the variation of
troop strength in the battle zone, S, with respect to time. For

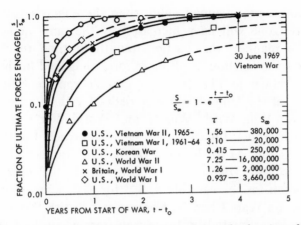

Figure 5a. Normalized battle strength expressed as the fraction of ultimate forces engaged plotted vs. years from the start of the war for the major U.S. wars.

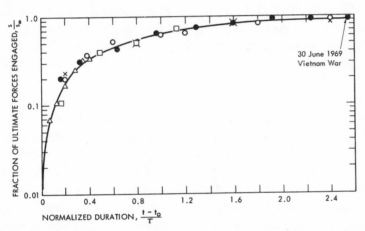

Figure 5b. Normalized battle strength plotted vs. normalized duration for each war analyzed.

the case of Vietnam War II, as shown in Fig. 4b, one finds that $\tau = 1.56$ years; i.e., in the first 1.56 years, sixty-three percent of the troops that are to be committed to the battle zone will have been committed. In the next 1.56 years, eighty-six percent of the troops will have been committed; and in the next 1.56 years (yields a total of 4.68 years), ninety-five percent of the ultimate forces will have been committed. If the coupling relationships are assumed valid, then the enemy's strength in the battle zone will have increased by the same percentages.

In like manner, the battle strength to time relationship, plotted as the fraction of ultimate forces engaged in the battle zone, is shown in Fig. 5a by a graphic representation of a summary of the United States statistics for the Vietnam War, the Korean War, World War II, and World War I (including the British army). Figure 5a has been constructed in the same manner as Fig. 4a in the light of the last equation. Here the strength of the United States Army in the battle zone has been chosen for the variable S. S_∞ for each war is estimated. For Vietnam Wars I and II, Korean, and British World War I, S_∞ can be estimated by inspection from a graph of strength versus time for each war in the same manner, as $S_\infty = 6000,000$ is observed for Department of Defense strength in Vietnam War II in Fig. 4a. The estimated value for the United States Army in these cases is as given in Fig. 5a.

Not so obvious is the ultimate strength that could have been mobilized by the United States in World War I and World War II. In these two cases, the wars ended before the curves became sufficiently horizontal to determine by inspection the value of S_∞. Thus, for World War II a value of sixteen million is chosen for S_∞, because this was estimated to be the absolute ceiling on the number of men who could be considered physically fit for active war service at that time.[26] Similarly, an S_∞ value of 3,670,000 was chosen for United States participation in World War I because it was the same percentage of our population in France as Great Britain's two million soldiers in France was of her total population in 1918.

If one choose arbitrarily the initial time, t_0, such that S_0/S_∞ is at least less than 0.10, the variation of S/S_∞ for the different wars can then be plotted, and is shown in Fig. 5a. The time constants for the different wars can then be determined. The exception of World War II should be noted where t_0 of June 1942 was chosen.

The last equation shows that $S(t - t_0)/S_\infty$ is the same function of the parameter $(t - t_0)/\tau$ for all wars. This means that all wars can be brought together and represented by a single line when S/S_∞ is plotted against $(t - t_0)/\tau$ for each war. That this is true, is shown in Fig. 5b for all wars analyzed.

This derivation and demonstration, in effect, shows that if the battle strength is expressed in terms of the percentage of ultimate forces to be engaged and is plotted against the time constant for each particular war, all wars studied can be expressed by a single mathematical relationship. Thus, each war forms a pattern over time and then history repeats each pattern.

Figure 5b allows comparison between the Vietnam War and all other wars analyzed. Where the Vietnam War stood, with respect to all other wars as of 30 June 1969, and every other six-month interval back to 30 June 1965, can be seen by the black data points. In summary, it can be seen that ninety percent of the troops to be committed by both sides had been committed by 30 June 1969. It can also be seen that the rate of change from now on should stay minimal, providing those conditions that have been acting over the past four years continue to act unchanged in the future.

Deviations of the actual data points from the theoretical curves can be traced to a number of causes, such as the effects of elections, weather, and influenza epidemics. However, the major phenomenon seen here is the remarkable stability and trueness-to-course that, in general, wars follow over long periods of time. Instead of great variability, which is the expected characteristic of the conduct of human affairs, the exact opposite condition seems to exist when the human affair is warfare. When viewed in the manner demonstrated here, wars appear to become remarkably orderly and mathematically lawful events.

Implications for the Vietnam War

Because of the orderliness of our behavior, the implication of the Vietnam data is that we, the United States, our allies, and our enemies, as of this writing, have reached a point in the

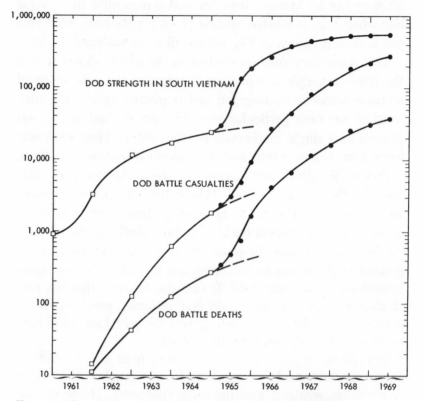

Figure 6. The vital statistics of the U.S. Department of Defense in South Vietnam plotted vs. time from December 1960 to 30 June 1969.

war where either a settlement is possible or another major escalation is indicated.

What prompts this statement is the shape of the curves for each of the previous wars and the shape of the curves for the Vietnam War. The shape of the curves for the past wars, and particularly the manner in which they level off, suggests that peace is negotiated when death, casualty, and strength exponentially approach the horizontal.

The overall leveling of these vital statistics can be seen in the British and German armies during World War I, leading to a conclusion in November 1918 and for the armies of the Union and Confederacy, leading to a conclusion in April

1865. The same leveling occurred in the Korean War, and led to a conclusion in July 1953. An identical pattern can be traced in the first phase of the Vietnam War, Fig. 6, which ended December 1964. It can be further noted that the Korean War and the Vietnam War are relatively close together in time and place; thus their comparability is best of all the other wars.

As of this writing, since most of the principal nations of the world are supplying money, material, men, or some combination of the three, indeed, in reality, a global decision period is at hand.

ACKNOWLEDGMENTS

For ideas and encouragement, I thank Mr. Sidney Burr Brinckerhoff, Fellow, Company of Military Historians; and Professors: Ronald Grant (Physiology), Ernest R. Hilgard (Psychology), Krishnamurty Karamcheti (Aeronautics and Astronautics), James McGregor (Mathematics), Robert C. North (Political Sciences, Studies of International Conflict and Integration) of Stanford University; and Dr. Samuel C. McIntosh, Research Associate, Aeronautics and Astronautics, Stanford University; and Dr. S. L. Waleszczak, Chief Scientist and RADM E. R. Zumwalt, Jr., Director, Systems Analysis Division, Office of the Chief of Naval Operations. For all interpretations of the data, however, I am solely responsible.

REFERENCES AND NOTES

1. S. S. Stevens, *Handbook of Experimental Psychology*, ed. S. S. Stevens (New York: John Wiley & Sons, 1966), pp. 1–49.
2. N. Wiener, *Cybernetics* (Cambridge: MIT, 1962), pp. 95–115.
3. L. F. Richardson, *Arms and Insecurity* (Pittsburgh: Boxwood, 1960), pp. 1–36.
4. F. W. Lanchester, *Aircraft in Warfare; The Dawn of the Fourth Arm* (London: Constable, 1916).
5. W. S. Churchill, *The World Crisis*, 3 (New York: Charles Scribner's Sons, 1924), p. 39.
6. T. L. Livermore, *Numbers and Losses in the Civil War in America: 1861–1865* (Bloomington: Indiana University Press, 1957), pp. 75–141.

7. Office of the Assistant Secretary of Defense (Public Affairs), "Vietnam Weekly Casualties, Statistical Summary" (Washington, D. C.: Department of Defense).

8. Office of the Comptroller of the Army, Program Review and Analysis Division, "ROK and UN Ground Forces Strength in Korea, 31 July 1950–31 July 1953" (Washington, D. C.: Department of Defense, 7 October 1954). Data is taken from Table 3.

9. "Annual Report of the Secretary of the Army–1948" (Washington, D. C.: Department of Defense, Government Printing Office, 1949), p. 295.

10. L. P. Ayres, *The War with Germany—A Statistical Summary* 1st Ed. (Washington, D. C.: Government Printing Office, 1919), p. 15.

11. *Ibid.*, p. 14.

12. Livermore, *Number and Losses*, p. 47.

13. Office of the Assistant Secretary of Defense (Public Affairs), "Vietnam Weekly." Only 1 percent of battle casualties are classified as missing and prisoners. This is the lowest percentage of all wars considered.

14. Office of the Assistant Chief of Staff, "Battle Casualties of the Army, 30 September 1954," CSGPA, 363 (Washington, D. C.: Department of the Army). Of all battle casualties recorded, approximately ten percent were listed as missing in action, captured, or returned.

15. Office of the Adjutant General, Statistical and Accounting Branch under the direction of the Program Review and Analysis Division of the Office of the Comptroller of the Army, *Army Battle Casualties and Non-Battle Deaths in World War II, 7 December 1941–31 December 1946*, OCS Report Control Symbol CSCAP-(OT)87 (Washington, D. C.: Department of the Army), pp. 10, 95. All theaters and campaigns, including the Army Air Corps officers and enlisted men, are grouped in U.S. Army casualties, except from 7 December 1941 to 10 May 1942. During this period three noncombat divisions were captured and held for the duration of the war. This resulted in 30,838 casualties and 13,847 deaths being listed as having occurred in the single month of May 1942. This accounting procedure thus caused the only significant statistical anomaly noted in all the data. Hence these data were excluded. About 9.3 percent of all battle casualties are classified as missing or captured.

16. Ayres, *War with Germany*, pp. 120–22. Battle deaths include only deaths from action. They do not include deaths from diseases and privation. Battle deaths for the month of May 1917 were estimated as 400, the month of April as 100, and the month of December as 800. With these estimates, a 4.4 percent difference exists between total battle deaths of 48,909 reported on page 122 and the accumulated total deaths on page 120. Total battle

casualties at the end of the war were 286,330, of which 7,347
were classified as missing in action or taken prisoner. The total
wounded was 230,074. The others were killed. As in the Vietnam
War, negligible casualties are classified as missing and prisoners,
about 2.6 percent. No reasonable explanation for this similarity
has been forthcoming.

17. The War Office, *Statistics of the Military Effort of the British Empire During the Great War, 1914–1920* (London: HM Stationery
Office, 1922), pp. 358–62. The British list a total of 2,441,673
casualties, including missing and prisoners, and 2,177,484, excluding missing and prisoners. Thus, approximately eleven percent of the total were classified as missing and prisoners. Similarly, the total German casualties, including missing and prisoners,
is 1,680,396, of which 1,313,421 were wounded and killed.
Thus, approximately twenty-two percent have been classified as
missing and prisoners mostly in the last year of the war. Finally,
comparative statistics between Great Britain and Germany are
not available for 1914. These data are assumed to be small in
comparison to the total losses.

18. W. S. Churchill, *World Crisis*, p. 39.

19. Livermore, *Numbers and Losses*, pp. 75–141. For certain battles,
listed on pages 140 and 141, Confederate strength on the battlefield for a particular battle (not battle strength) had to be estimated and was assumed to be one-half of the known Union
strength. This in general proved to be the case throughout the
war. Estimates of Confederate battle casualties, when their
derivation was necessary, were made by multiplying the Confederate battlefield strength by 0.123, which is the average Confederate casualty per soldier engaged in thirty battles of which
twelve were defeats and eighteen were victories. Estimates of
Confederate battle deaths, when made necessary, were derived
by multiplying Confederate battle casualties for that battle by
17.6 percent, which is the average for twenty-nine battles. Estimates of Union battle deaths were made by multiplying Union
battle casualties by 17.5 percent, which is the average for thirty-
seven battles. Union and Confederate missing, and prisoners, were
not available.

20. J. Voevodsky, "Quantitative Behavior of Warring Nations," *Journal
of Psychology* 72 (1969): 269–92.

21. G. C. Marshall, *Biannual Report to the Chief of Staff of the U.S.
Army, July 1, 1943–June 30, 1945* (Washington, D. C.: Government Printing Office, 1945), p. 101.

22. Lieutenant General Nicholas Golovine, *The Russian Army in the
World War* (New Haven, Conn.: Yale University Press; Oxford:
Oxford University Press, 1931).

23. J. Voevodsky, *Behavioral Cybernetics* (San Jose, Cal.: Spartan Book
Store, 1970).

170

24. J. Voevodsky, "A Mathematical Representation of Time-Variant Quantitative Behavior," *Journal of Psychology* 68 (1968): 129–40.

25. J. Voevodsky, et. al., "The Measurement of Suprathreshold Pain," *American Journal of Psychology* 80 (1967): 124-28.

26. Marshall, G. E., "Biannual Report."

Computer Simulation – Gospel, Guidance, or Garbage

STANLEY WINKLER

Executive Office of the President
Washington, D. C.

Introduction

There can be no doubt about the universal appeal of simulation in our society. I personally believe that this universal appeal stems from the apparent simplicity of the technique. Anyone can do it. It is tempting to recall the proverb which says, "Simplicity is the sign of truth—and of fallacy."[1]

Please do not misunderstand. I am in favor of simulation. Let the cynics decry the production of large volumes of waste paper, and let the detractors belittle those who run out of ideas long before they run out of machine time. I would argue that there is much good and little harm in the large volume of simulation currently in vogue. Nevertheless, I must confess that I was startled when, in response to my request for a bibliography on simulation covering the last few years, I received a box two feet high filled with 14" x 11" printouts, including abstracts. I have learned to phrase my requests more carefully. To this audience, there is no need to belabor the point about the ubiquitousness of simulations. The proliferation of simulation languages and simulation packages is eloquent evidence.[2] Can there be anything, real or imaginary, within the human span which has not been simulated?

I do not want to enter the semantic morass of definitions of

171

simulation. For the purposes of this paper, I assume we can agree that in a general, imprecise sense simulation is a technique for representing "reality" by a model which can be manipulated in a digital computer and whose computer behavior reasonably approximates "reality" within the framework of interest.

The Structure of a Simulation

Before outlining the structure of a simulation, I would like to make several distinctions. First, I want to recognize that there is a "difference between a successful simulation and an incoherent attempt to program one's own ignorance."[3] The point I want to make is that successful computer simulation is not inherently simple. Careful, sophisticated consideration must be given to all aspects of each simulation, if the costly production of nonsense outputs is to be avoided. Moss[4] stated this very well when he expressed

> . . . the need both for increasing sophistication on the part of those who approach simulation techniques on the "last-resort" basis, and for more analysis of the problems associated with the compromise that must be made between naïve, workable simplicity, and sophisticated, unmanageable complexity.

Second, I want to distinguish between simulation and numerical analysis. Numerical analysis includes the strategy of computation as well as the evaluation of the results.[5] I am not opposed to numerical analysis, either. It's just that there is more to simulation than numerical analysis even if you believe, as many do, that simulation is a numerical technique.[6] From my viewpoint, numerical analysis is a tool used in performing the operations in a simulation. Mistaking the tool (or a set of tools) for the simulation leads to erroneous emphasis on the *how* rather than the *what* of a simulation. Sometimes, as Cyert remarks, this mistake is not entirely accidental.[7] There is a mystique surrounding the word *simulation*, and its use invokes the image of modern, advanced capabilities. Therefore some individuals, intent on placing their wares in a most favorable light, refer to simple, albeit tedious, calculations as a simulation. Let us not be too harsh on such individuals. Not only may such computations be very useful, but these individuals are really on the right track. One should never do a simulation when a calculation will suffice.

Finally, I want to mention some of the ways in which simulations may be classified. One way is based on time, and thus we can distinguish between discrete event or variable time-step calculations and continuous or fixed time-step simulations. The variable time-step method permits the processing to depend on the successive occurrence of discrete events and on the corresponding decisions associated with them. The fixed time-step method is appropriate for continuous systems which are generally describable by differential equations. The analyst may have the option of selecting either method, and the choice will affect the amount of computer time required for the problem.[8]

Another basis for classification is the nature of the simulation output. The output might be a description of organizational behavior or another dynamic process, or the output might be comparison of alternative courses of action. Cyert identifies four classes of simulations of organizational behavior, which he characterizes as descriptive studies of existing organizations, illustrative studies of hypothetical organizations, normative studies for organizational design, and man-machine studies for training.[9] Simulation is well suited to the evaluation of a sequence of alternatives. Conway states that simulation can obtain "relative results much more efficiently than absolute results."[10]

Let us now examine the structure of a simulation. A simple view is shown in Fig. 1. In this figure, I identify four operations as central to a simulation:

1. model building
2. manipulation (of the model)
3. interpretation (of the results)
4. comparison (with "reality").

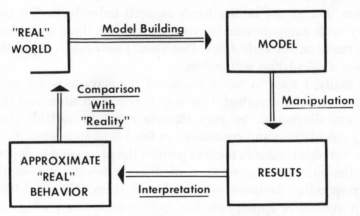

Figure 1. A simple view of simulation.

Of the four operations, manipulation of the model has received the greatest amount of attention. Model building has been discussed competently and in detail by a number of authors, but the belief is still widespread that any problem can be readily programmed for a computer if only a good programmer is available. Lip service is always paid to the comparison with reality, and certainly everyone is aware that this is a good thing to do. The necessity for careful, considered interpretation or translation of the results of manipulating the model is frequently overlooked. I would like to examine each of these operations in a little more detail.

Model Building

Model building is a difficult art. In the first place, the model is an abstraction and should contain only enough detail to facilitate obtaining the desired results. But how much is "enough"? Many people naïvely believe that if more detail is included in the model, the simulation results automatically will be better or at least more accurate (whatever *better* and *accurate* may mean). This is not true, and unfortunately there is no simple rule for an analyst to apply. The best advice is, "use

1. KNOW THE PROBLEM

2. STATE ALL ASSUMPTIONS

3. DETERMINE INPUT DATA

4. SPECIFY OUTPUT

5. ESTIMATE USE

Figure 2. Some rules for model building.

good judgment!" and as you know, good judgment is learned only from many bad experiences. In the second place, there is the practical problem of balancing the costs of a simulation, that is, the cost of building the model, writing the program, running the computer, and interpreting the results, as well as the cost of collecting and inputting the required data. And in the third place, it may not be possible to build a satisfactory model. This last statement may sound like heresy, and I must admit that I have never heard of anyone who failed to run a large simulation because a satisfactory model could not be built.

Although model building is difficult, and I suspect that many of the most successful model builders use an intuitive approach, there are some rules which may be helpful. These are shown in Fig. 2.

The first rule is to know the problem that is to be solved and to understand the questions for which answers are desired. An understanding of the problem under study permits the meaningful introduction of simplifications and the elimination of detail which may exist in the real situation but which is unessential to the simulation. It is important that the designer of a simulation know the purpose of the model he is building. A successful simulation must answer the questions asked, and an efficient one must also avoid unnecessary and unwanted details.

The second rule is to state all the assumptions made in constructing the model. It is perhaps inevitable that some assumptions will be made tacitly and not be recognized explicitly. A knowledge of the underlying assumptions is necessary to understand the limitations and approximations introduced by the model. Acceptance of a model is often determined by the extent to which the underlying assumptions are explicitly stated.

The third rule is to determine the requirements for input data. A simulation model is incomplete if the input data necessary to run the simulation cannot be obtained. In this connection, it is important to note that past or historical data may be inadequate, even if available, when the problem concerns future events. The generation of appropriate input data is sometimes a major difficulty and can be the most critical item in a simulation.

The fourth rule is to specify the output in terms of the precision desired and the level of detail required in the model to achieve this.

The fifth rule is to estimate the use of the model. The use will be an important input to any decision to improve the model and increase its efficiency. The intended use of a model will also help in deciding on the amount of flexibility to build into it.

The validity of a model is hard to establish, and it should be remembered that a model may resemble a real situation but not actually behave like the real thing. In most cases, a determination of the validity of the model must await the pragmatic test of how well it serves the purpose for which it was intended. Naylor and Finger[11] have discussed this problem in some detail. They suggest a multistage approach to the verification of a simulation model in which the analyst rationalizes the assumptions which underlie the model, attempts to verify these assumptions on some basis or other, and, to the extent possible, tests the ability of the model to predict the behavior of the operation or system being simulated. Cyert suggests that "a good deal of judgment must enter into the evaluation

1. Construct Flow Charts

2. Formulate Algorithms

3. Do An Error Analysis

4. Design The Experiment

5. Program And Run The Computer

Figure 3. Manipulation of the model.

of computer models." He also lists eight measures for testing the "goodness of fit" of a model.[12]

The verification of a model is closely connected with the validity of the simulation. A number of authors recommend checking the predictive capability of a simulation against historical data. I shall illustrate this later with an econometric model. However, comparison with historical data indicates plausibility but does not necessarily demonstrate validity.

Manipulation of the Model

The manipulation of the model is not entirely separate and distinct from the development of the model itself. When formulating the model, the designer must have in mind how he intends to proceed. The choice of the programming language, the kind of numerical analyses, and the nature of the sampling techniques used are not independent of the model. Figure 3 lists the five operational steps which constitute the manipulation of the model. Steps 2, 3, and 4 may be grouped under the heading of numerical analysis.

In essence, numerical analysis consists of the formation of algorithms; error analysis, including truncation and roundoff error; the study of convergence, including the rate of convergence; and comparative algorithms, which judge the relative utility of different algorithms in different situations.[13] Monte

Carlo methods are considered to be included within this structuring of numerical analysis. The term *Monte Carlo simulation* is found frequently in the literature. From the viewpoint adopted here, Monte Carlo is considered a technique useful in but different from *simulation*. Variance reduction is an important aspect of Monte Carlo methods.[14]

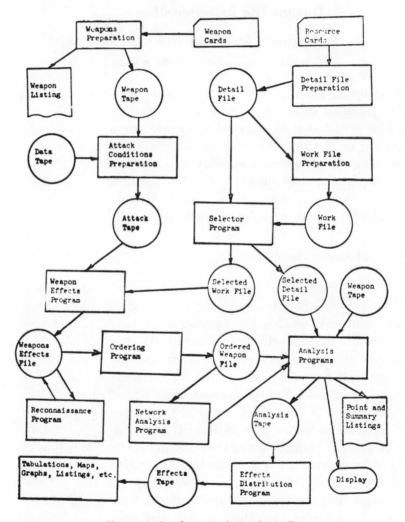

Figure 4. Combat simulation-logic flow.

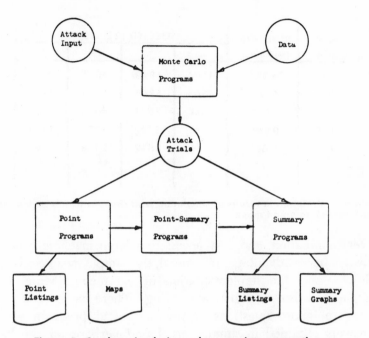

Figure 5. Combat simulation subsystem interconnection.

To put it another way, numerical analysis furnishes the procedure by which some kind of an answer is obtained and, by means of the error analysis, helps decide whether the answer is any good or not. Convergence theory considers the question of whether answers can be improved, given a particular type of algorithm.

Sampling is an important part of any simulation experiment. Techniques, which long have been familiar to statisticians, can be invoked to improve the information which can be obtained from a limited amount of experimentation, and I suspect that many of the simulations currently being performed would benefit considerably from good experimental design. There have been a number of interesting papers published on the statistical analysis of simulation experiments.[15] This is a good place to recall the fact that a large digital computer is not required for

STEP SIZE	RUN TIME (Seconds)	SELECTED RESULTS			
		A	B	C	D
0.05	16.076	4567	5848	4095	4610
0.5	6.124	4565	5844	4094	4573
1.0	5.075	4561	5837	4093	4526
10.0	0.941	1787	3722	2393	5272
15.0	0.880	1776	3642	2338	4785

Figure 6. Variation in results of simulation with changes in step size using a differential equation model.

every simulation, and easy access to a large machine may not always be an advantage. In general, the sample mean converges slowly, and the implementation of variance-reducing techniques can provide significant savings. There has been a tendency to ignore questions of reliability and precision of the answers obtained in simulations, based perhaps on the hope that all problems will yield to a large enough expenditure of machine time.

The question of whether the flow charts are part of the model or an operation in manipulating the model is to some extent a matter of taste. My own preference is given here. The charts themselves may be very detailed or highly aggregated. Two charts used in programming a combat simulation are shown in Figs. 4 and 5.

Programming and running the computer sounds like a routine operation which can be passed to the computer group and forgotten. I would caution the analyst to avoid thinking that any portion of a simulation may be safely considered routine. In Fig. 6, the variation in results with different step sizes dramatically demonstrates the necessity of being "eternally vigilant." This is a case in which a step size of 10.0 was initially selected in order to save CPU time and reduce costs.

Clearly, of the sizes presented in the figure, a step size of 1.0 is indicated, while a smaller size is unwarranted. This is just another illustration of the basic doctrine that successful simulations are the result of continuous and careful attention to every element and operation.

Interpretation of Results

Having built a model and processed a large number of computer runs, the next problem is to do something with the avalanche of paper produced by the computer. Do not underestimate the ability of a large-scale modern computer to produce paper. One of the bright young scientists in our office calculated that, if the forward edge of the paper pouring out of our high-speed printer were ignited, the flame front would not reach the printer operating at its rated speed. There are times when this instant incineration seems like a real good idea. But, assuming that the simulation experiments have been designed properly and that the results obtained have been carefully prepared to contain only useful summarized informa-

● COLLECT SIMULATION DATA
- Select Format
- Do Additional Calculations
- Summarize

●PERFORM STATISTICAL ANALYSIS
- Mean, Variance
- Tests of Hypotheses
- Multiply Comparisons
- Spectral Analysis

●EXAMINE THE DATA
- A Priori Reasonableness
- Sensitivity to Input Changes
- Look for Discontinuities
- Compare with Expected Results

Figure 7. Interpreting the result.

- TABULATIONS
- GRAPHS
- MAPS
- STATEMENTS
- INPUTS TO OTHER SIMULATIONS

Figure 8. Simulation outputs.

tion, there remains the job of interpretation or translating the results of manipulation of the model into a reasonable and useful approximation of the real world. As I stated earlier, I believe this an aspect of the simulation process which is most often neglected. One should not carry out an actual simulation without having decided beforehand how the results are to be interpreted and evaluated. By evaluation, I mean the detailed consideration of the results in relation to the problem which was to be solved.

A suggested orderly procedure for the interpretation of the results of a simulation is shown in Fig. 7. The output of a simulation can be presented in a number of ways. Five of the most common of these are listed in Fig. 8. The analyst should select the type or types of outputs which will facilitate the interpretation of the results of the simulation.

In translating the results of a simulation, one, of course, has the full storehouse of statistical techniques and numerical analysis to call upon.[16] Here again is a place to exercise caution. Fishman and Kiviat point out that simulation data are generally autocorrelated, but that most users have either ignored the existence of autocorrelation or have inadequately accounted for it.[17] This paper discusses in detail the use of spectral analysis for analyzing the results of a simulation. The comparison of the autocorrelation structure of two processes provides more insight than a comparison of their means.

Careful examination of the data generated by a simulation

is always a useful exercise. If the data does not appear to be reasonable, and if the results obtained are not close to those which were expected, then a further study of the bases of the simulation is highly desirable. Here again, experience is a helpful but not infallible guide. There is an unfortunate tendency on the part of experienced analysts to sometimes explain away an unexpected result, only later to learn that the rejected result was meaningful.

Equally important is a grasp of the underlying processes which the simulation attempts to describe. The conclusions which can be reached depend not only upon the numerical results obtained, but also upon an understanding of these underlying processes. I think it important that the analyst make an explicit distinction between conclusions which can be supported by a logical interpretation of the results, and hypotheses which are made plausible by the results of the simulation. This may appear to be a trivial or self-evident point, but I think the distinction between supportable conclusions and plausible guesses is not often as clear as it might be.

Comparison with Reality

The true test of the simulation is, of course, its ability to predict observable events in the real world. As changes or stresses are introduced into the simulation, the resultant be-

THUROW MODEL : Macro-economic model for long range policy impact evaluation.

● **EXOGENOUS VARIABLES**   44

23 POLICY INSTRUMENTS
21 INDEPENDENTLY FORECAST

● **ENDOGENOUS VARIABLES**   62

Figure 9. Econometric model.

havior should approximate the corresponding behavior of the "real" system. Whenever it is possible, the simulated data should be compared with actual data. But a simulation would not be necessary if actual data were available; therefore, in most instances direct comparisons with real data cannot be made. It is easy to illustrate this point. A few examples where simulation can be used to answer questions for which real data are not easily obtained are:

1. prediction of economic performance over the next five years
2. analysis of a manned space mission
3. determination of the load conditions under which a telephone system would break down.

	1968	1968 Actual	% Diff.
GROSS NATIONAL PRODUCT	697.7	707.6	1.4
PERSONAL INCOME	563.1	590.0	4.6
GROSS INVESTMENT	75.7	75.9	0.3
PERSONAL CONSUMPTION	433.1	452.6	4.3
DIVIDENDS	22.1	23.1	4.4
LABOR FORCE	80.0	82.3	2.8

Figure 10. Comparison of predicted with actual values using an economic model.

An econometric model, which is currently being studied, is the Thurow model, whose gross characteristics are shown in Fig. 9. The Thurlow model is a macroeconomic model designed for the evaluation of the long range impact of policy decisions. The coefficients for the equations used in this model were developed on the basis of historical data. Using this model, predictions were made for the values of six economic

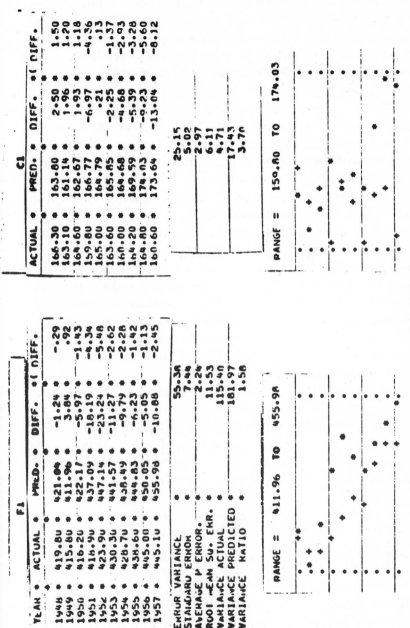

Figure 11. Simulation outputs.

indicators for the year 1968. These are shown in Fig. 10, together with the actual values.[18] As can be seen, the agreement
between predicted and actual values is good. Whether or not
future predicitions would be equally good depends on how
smoothly and gradually the changes in the national economic
situation take place.

Figure 11 depicts the output of another econometric simulation for two of the variables: consumer expenditure for food,
F1, and consumer expenditure for clothing, C1. The values
under the column labelled PRED. are those produced by the
simulation for the years 1948 through 1957. The actual values
are shown for comparison in the column labelled ACTUAL,
under DIFF. are the differences, and under (DIFF., the percentages of the differences are listed. In the same figure, some
statistical measures are listed, and guide graphs of the variables F1 and C1 are plotted by the on-line computer printer,
with the values of F1 and C1 as the abscissa, and the dates in
ascending order as the ordinate. The + represent the predicted
or simulation values while the * represent the actual or historical values. The simulation was performed using a quadratic
utility function.[19] Here again, in my judgment, the comparisons
appear to be satisfactory.

As I mentioned before, the fact that the results of a simulation compared favorably with actual data in the past does
not *guarantee* that future predictions will be equally good.
Nonetheless, such comparisons are useful, with good results
supporting the validity of the simulation, and poor results
indicating difficulties. Van Horn writes that

> validation is the process of building an acceptable level of confidence
> that an inference about a simulated process is a correct or valid
> inference for the actual process. Seldom, if ever, will validation
> result in "proof" that the simulator is a correct or "true" model of
> the real process.[20]

If the validity of the simulation is to be established, the
output of a simulation must be compared with reality, if only
in an approximate way. Often this cannot be done, and the

pragmatic decision to accept the results of a simulation as valid may depend upon the demonstrable care with which the simulation was constructed and conducted, and also upon the past history of success or failure with similar simulations.

Interactive Simulation

I have discussed the structure of simulation together with some of the difficulties and problems encountered. I have tried to indicate some of the precautions to be observed by those who would simulate in earnest. I should like now to connect simulation with the theme of this conference "Cybernetics in the Seventies." Prophesying future developments is a tricky business, and therefore I will talk only about those things which are under development today. The remote interactive terminal, which is now becoming more readily available, will introduce significant changes both in the nature of simulations and in the use that can be made of them.

We are currently experimenting with two modes of inter-action for simulations. The first is in connection with the performance of simulation itself. A number of decision points can be inserted in the simulation, and the intervention of the analyst, if required, can be requested at an appropriate place in the simulation. Since we operate with a number of terminals at remote locations, we not only can provide convenient intervention by a single individual, but we have the option of obtaining a consensus of expert opinion, and then inserting an average or a weighted average. The exciting possibility of not having to specify decision rules in advance of intermediate results will make a significant change in simulation procedures. The second exciting possibility with which we are experimenting is the ability to complete a simulation and, using remote interactive queries, obtain selected results. We have successfully done this with a very large simulation, allowing ten individuals with different interests to utilize simultaneously the results of the simulation. Built into this program is the capability of performing additional simulation and additional calculations. We have available for this two appropriately specialized processors. One, a time-series processor which conveniently manipulates rows and columns, and performs the recursion analysis. The other is a matrix arithmetic package which does matrix inversion and other matrix operations.

We also have an experimental version of an econometric model. In using this, a nonprogrammer can sit at a terminal and insert values for policy instruments over a simulated time period of years, with the ability to review the results on a quarterly or annual basis. I can become very excited about this form of interactive econometrics, not only as an aid to the policy maker himself, but as an extremely flexible training device. The instructor from the privacy of his office can monitor the performance of a group of students working on their own terminals. He can also inject comments or change some of the parameters in the simulation for the benefit of any individual student.

As human interaction with simulation becomes more convenient, the capabilities become limited only by imagination. Let me emphasize that what I have just mentioned is not what we hope to do in the future, but what we are doing currently in a small experimental way. I believe that the major technical and programming difficulties have been overcome, and that the remaining problems are those of deciding what, in fact, is useful and worthwhile doing. How much further we develop these tasks, and to what extent they will be utilized, depend on the assigning of priorities and the nature of the problems to be solved. As usual in science, one must ask the right questions to get useful answers.

Concluding Remarks

Simulation has had a long and honorable history. Sir Isaac Newton used simulation on a grand—shall I say, universal— scale. He built a mathematical model and used this model to compute the motion of celestial bodies. Similarly, computer simulation arises in a very natural way from scientific practice.

The electronic analog computer has been used to simulate a large variety of systems, following in the footsteps of earlier, mechanical differential analyzers. And so it was natural and to be expected that the digital computer would be used for simulation. Today, as more practitioners develop greater expertise, computer simulation is moving from an *art* to a structured technique with known strengths and limitations.

But it must always be true that, by itself, computer simulation is neither good nor bad, right nor wrong. It is the user who determines whether computer simulations produce gospel, guidance, or garbage.

ACKNOWLEDGMENTS

I want to express my appreciation to my friends and colleagues who so generously helped in the formulation of the ideas presented here. In particular I want to thank Richard H. Wilcox, David O. Wood, Nathaniel Macon, Carl Hammer, Joseph Correia, and Mrs. Harriette Wade for their many kindnesses and assistance in the preparation of this paper.

REFERENCES

1. K. Lorenz, quoted by L. Berkowitz, *American Scientist*, 57, no. 3 (1969): 372.
2. T. H. Naylor, "ACM Bibliography 19, Simulation and Gaming," *Computing Reviews*, 10, no. 1 (January 1969): and J. F. Lubin, "Computer Simulation—Discussion of the Technique and Comparison of Languages," *Communications of the ACM*, 9, no. 10 (1966): 723–41.
3. J. Harling, "Simulation Techniques in Operations Research—A Review," *Journal of Operations Research*, 6, no. 3 (1958): 307–19.
4. J. H. Moss, "Commentary on Harling's 'Simulation Techniques in Operations Research,'" *Journal of Operations Research*, 6, no. 4 (1958): 591–93.
5. P. J. Davis, "Numerical Analysis," *The Mathematical Sciences: Essays for COSRIMS* (Cambridge, Mass.: M.I.T. Press, 1969), pp. 128–37.
6. T. H. Naylor et al., *Computer Simulation Techniques* (New York: John Wiley & Sons, 1966), p. 3.

190 STANLEY WINKLER

7. R. M. Cyert, "A Description and Evaluation of Some Firm Simulations," *Proceedings of the IBM Scientific Computing Symposium on Simulation Models and Gaming* (1966), p. 4.
8. Naylor, *Computer Simulation*, pp. 126–27.
9. Cyert, "Some Firm Simulations," pp. 4–5.
10. R. W. Conway, "Some Tactical Problems in Digital Simulation," *Management Science*, 10 (October 1963): 13.
11. T. H. Naylor and J. M. Finger, "Verification of Computer Simulation Models," *Management Science*, 14, no. 2 (October 1967): B92–B106.
12. Cyert, "Some Firm Simulations," pp. 17–18.
13. Davis, "Numerical Analysis," pp. 128–37.
14. H. Kahn, "Use of Different Monte Carlo Sampling Techniques," P–766 (November 1955), Rand Corporation. See also, J. M. Hammersley and D. C. Handscomb, *Monte Carlo Methods* (New York: John Wiley & Sons, 1964).
15. G. S. Fishman, "Problems in Statistical Analysis of Simulation Experiments: The Comparison of Means and Sample Records," *Communications of the ACM*, 10, no. 2 (February 1967): 94–99. Also, D. S. Burdick and T. H. Naylor, "Design of Computer Simulation Experiments for Industrial Systems," *Communications of the ACM*, 9, no. 5, (May 1966): 329–39. And T. H. Naylor, D. S. Burdick, and W. E. Sasser, "Computer Simulation Experiments with Economic Systems: The Problem of Experimental Design," *Journal of the American Statistical Association*, 62 (December 1967): 1315–37.
16. T. H. Taylor, K. Wertz, and T. H. Wonnacott, "Methods for Analyzing Data from Computer Simulation Experiments," *Communications of the ACM*, 10, no. 11 (November 1967): 703–10.
17. G. S. Fishman and P. J. Kiviat, "The Analysis of Simulation-Generated Time Series," *Management Science*, 13, no. 7 (March 1967): 526.
18. D. O. Wood, Private communication.
19. *Ibid.*
20. R. Van Horn, "Validation," *The Design of Computer Simulation Experiments*, ed. T. H. Naylor (Durham, N. C.: Duke University Press, 1969), 2330.

IV
The Technology:
Cybernetics in the Seventies and Beyond

Information Systems
in the Seventies

RICHARD D. LEVÉE

Control Data Corporation
Minneapolis, Minnesota

Over the past few years Marshall McLuhan has been exploring the concept of hot and cool media. Hot media are low in participation or completion by the audience and cool media are high. For example, McLuhan suggests that television, which is a cool medium, becomes rather warm when viewing baseball because it is difficult for the viewer to become involved in a game of one-thing-at-a-time—fixed positions and visibly delegated specialist jobs. On the other hand, football is very cool. All twenty-two players are intimately involved in every play. There is a switching of roles, a greater need for strategy, and every spectator can be an armchair quarterback. Because football allows the audience to participate more fully than other sports it has become *the major* TV sports event.

Now, in general, lectures are hot because of a lack of audience participation. However, I understand that last year at your second annual symposium some members of the audience did participate. In fact, the participation came when Chuck Purcell, also of Control Data, was the speaker. Therefore, in accord with this precedent and to cool down this talk, I'd like to ask you to participate again today by playing a small game with me.

I am going to flash a new slide on the screen in a moment,

and I would like you to write down the first word or group
of words that you associate with what is on the screen. O.K.?
Here it is. Now, let's see what some of your associations were
with the words *Information System.*

How many of you wrote down something like "face to face
communication"? How many of you thought of "television"?
How many of "videotape"? How many of the "telephone" or
some form of data communication network like the CYBER-
NET?* How many of some sort of "microfilm" system? How
many of an "electronic data processing system"? How many of
you wrote down something similar to an "on-line interactive
CRT or TTY terminal system"? And finally, how many of you
associated *Information System* with cybernetics?

Now these are only a few of the many possible things one
might associate with *Information System,* but over the past
year, I have asked a lot of people the same question, and, almost invariably, their association has been with either an EDP
system or an on-line interactive system. Clearly, these *are* important ingredients of today's information systems, but if we
hope to cope with the information needs of the seventies, we
are going to have to discard the blinders, expand our views,
and develop information systems with a cybernetic approach—
an approach in which the relationship between the information
and the user (decision making management) is an integral
part of system design. An approach in which accurate, relevant, timely information is supplied *as required* with lowest
cost and highest effectiveness.

Now, it is this cybernetic approach to information systems
that I would like to explore with you today. First, I would like
to review briefly some of the needs that are arising for a vast
improvement of our information systems in the seventies. Then,
I would like to explore some of the directions in which improvements can take place, and finally suggest the direction
in which development is likely to take place.

That information systems are important is illustrated by A.

---

*Cybernet™ Service is Control Data Corporation's nation-wide network of
data centers and public and private terminals.

M. McDonough's comment that, " . . . some fifty percent of the costs of running our economy are information costs."[1] There are at least five areas where needs are developed which insure that a great improvement of our information systems will take place.

First, we have development of larger, more complex organizations, some involving vast decentralization.

Second, is the rapid growth of our corporations and the large number of acquisitions and mergers.

Third, we are in the midst of an information *explosion* caused mainly by three factors. One, the rapid growth of white collar workers from twenty-nine million in 1960, to forty-two million in 1970, to over fifty million in 1980. Two, the accelerating growth of output produced by computers, which numbered some 40,000 in 1968 and are expected to number 110,000 by 1978, and the power of which may well expand by a factor of sixteen by 1978 for a potential increase in output by a factor of something like fifty by 1980. With a production of some hundred billion computer printer pages per year today, this will mean a potential of tens of trillions of pages per year by 1980. A third factor in the information explosion is the acceleration in growth of dissemination of information by duplicators and copiers. The number of copies so produced will increase from about a trillion per year in 1970 to over ten trillion per year in 1980 if left unchecked.

Fourth, we are also in the midst of an information *implosion* caused by faster communication and reduced decision time.

Finally, there is increasing competition, a cooling economy, and a resultant profit squeeze which can be offset to a considerable extent by reduction in information costs.

Now, what are some of the directions or dimensions in which information systems can develop? I would like to describe three—system concepts, system processes, and system resources.

First, concepts: G. W. Dickson[2] has recently expanded and restructured the conceptual levels of information systems of Leavitt and Whisler[3] to arrive at the following five levels.

Level one—clerical systems. Most of the advances to date in

information systems have been made in this area, and the results have been impressive. Nevertheless, the basic concept here is *data processing*, and the output is, in general, a vast sea of numbers.

Unfortunately, most of the output provided by clerical systems is not directly useful for management decision making. Thus, the second level is one in which *information* is generated rather than data and which is structured for *decision making* by a *particular user*.

Third level systems are called *decision systems* because they concentrate on the *decision* process rather than on producing information necessary for the decision process. The techniques involved include economic and financial analysis, analysis for planning and control, mathematical modeling, resource allocation and cost-benefit analysis.

Level four systems are *interactive systems*. These systems concentrate on *cybernated* interaction—an interaction in which the decision maker and the information system are integrated into a problem-solving network.

Programmed systems are represented in level five. In these systems, the human is removed from the decision-making process, and this function is performed by the system. Few such systems exist, and most of the action at this level today is in the research phase.

In a second dimension, we have room for improvement of information systems by a consideration of *all* the basic processes involved.

The collection process might be *data oriented* like transactors, the key punch, the key cassette and the CRT, or it might be *information oriented* like the camera, which is a fantastically efficient collector of information.

The storage process can be *data oriented* like magnetic tapes, disk storage drives, disk files, and punch cards; or *information oriented* like paper, microfilm, and video tape.

A third process, the processing of data, can be very efficiently carried out by a fantastic assortment of computers of various capabilities and price.

The *data* retrieval process is carried out by line printers, card punches, CRTs, and TTYs in combination with the computer, and the *information* retrieval process is performed by attractive girls, manual and automated microfilm readers, and video file systems.

Finally, we have the dissemination function. Here we have mail, common carriers, CRTs, TTYs, paper, microfilm readers, and television.

To these five, we should add the functions of filing, summarization or analysis of the information retrieved, and user feedback.

A third dimension which can lead to improvement of information systems can be labeled *resources*. By expanding the types of products, people, and facilities we use in meeting the requirements of the system level and system functions, we can both reduce cost and increase effectiveness.

Now, in what direction in these three dimensions will the development of information systems take place in the seventies?

In the dimension of system level, the *sixties* were the era of *clerical data processing*. As the applications for clerical systems level off, and as the five information problems mentioned earlier become more acute, information system development will turn to improving the effectiveness of management decisions by properly structured information, decision systems, and interactive systems. Thus, the *seventies* will be the era of *cybernated information systems* where the *user* becomes a key factor in the design of the system. And, since the emphasis will be on information rather than data, we will need to develop a much better understanding of management information content, form, media, and timeliness.

Conclusion

In the late fifties and early sixties, the emphasis in information system functions was on data processing. Since the mid-sixties, there has been increasing emphasis on data collection, storage, retrieval, and dissemination. In line with the *clerical level* concept, the emphasis has been on *data*. As information systems people have turned their thoughts toward information rather than data, it has become obvious that to treat all information like data is costly and ineffective. Thus, today there is considerable development going on in the areas of *information* storage and retrieval and this development will be extended to the areas of *information* collection and dissemination in the seventies.

In the dimension of resources we have people, facilities, and products to consider. Already information system specialties and managers are beginning to appear, and this trend will continue to grow in the seventies. *Internal* information centers are also beginning to appear and with them the necessary personnel to support such a service function. These centers are analogous to the internal data processing centers which appeared in the sixties to handle the clerical information system function. *External* information centers are sure to develop, but here the time scale is not so clear because of the early stage of development of information systems beyond the clerical level. However, I would expect to see such utilities in the latter half of the 1970s.

Finally, we come to the products to be used in these second, third, and fourth level information-decision systems. It appears that, at least through the seventies, microfilm will be the major medium for *information* storage and that *microfilm and computer will be integrated* into highly efficient systems. The only other product available today which might compete with microfilm is the video file, but today's high cost precludes its extensive usage in the next few years.

The advances in microfilm have been impressive over the past few years, and a marriage to the computer has already taken place with the computer-output-microfilm product. Not only is microfilm output from computers faster and cheaper than conventional printers, but it can also be more effective because of graphic, variable size character and image overlay capability. Such products are now being manufactured by about twenty companies.

Integrated computer/microfilm storage and retrieval systems are just beginning to appear. These systems take advantage of the computer's ability to find out where certain information is stored, and the microfilm systems' ability to *store* information cheaply and effectively and to retrieve any page of this information from many thousands in three or four seconds. During the seventies, microfilm/computer information systems will be developed with considerably more capability in microfilm capacity, retrieval time, on-line collection, and on-line dissemination and updating. Such integrated systems promise to assist tremendously in the development of effective information systems.

To summarize, the development of information systems in the seventies will concentrate on those levels of information systems which directly involve the decision-making manager—his specific needs, his decision rules, or his interaction. The emphasis in the early seventies will be on storage and retrieval extending to other areas later on. By concentrating on user requirements the advantages of computers and microfilm will be married into single systems with greatly improved cost-effectiveness. So, even though emphasis today is still on data systems, there are a few who recognize that information systems require a much broader view of needs, processses, and products, and who will lead the way to the seventies as the era of *true information systems*.

REFERENCES

1. A. M. McDonough, *Information Economics and Management Systems* (New York: McGraw-Hill, 1963), p. 11.
2. G. W. Dickson, "Management Information-Decision Systems," *Business Horizons*, December 1968, p. 17.
3. H. J. Leavitt and T. L. Whisler, "Management in the 1980's," *Harvard Business Review*, November–December 1958, p. 41.

The Future: Interactive Electronic Systems

CARL HAMMER

Univac
Washington, D. C.

Scientists the world over are facing an awesome responsibility as their work brings them ever closer to the point where drastic and possibly irreversible changes in our earthly environment are taking effect. Some of these alterations, such as in the temperature of our atmosphere or of the oceans, result from the increasing pollution which our engineering technology produces. Other changes could result from planned experiments of a global nature; these might include redistribution of the water on the surface of the earth, or an attempt to control weather and climate over cities and even continents.

The solution of these and other problems of similar magnitude will require the application of electronic computer systems to a degree which by far exceeds their seemingly miraculous powers of today. Scarcely two hundred years ago, the German-Swiss mathematician Leonhard Euler completed his calculation of π to 600 decimals and concluded this Herculean effort with the laconic remark that "it would be impossible" to extend this computation further because of the excessive amount of manpower needed. He made this statement on the basis of the technology known to him in his own time. Yet, in the past twenty years, we have computed π first to 2,000, then to 10,000, and finally to 100,000 decimals!

201

For the record, the last computation took less than eight hours on one of our electronic brains, while Euler toiled for two years to finish his work by hand. Therefore, let us beware of attaching the label of impossibility to achievements whose implementation we can not readily foresee! After all, space travel, atomic energy, color television, and global communications, to mention just a few, were unheard of only fifty years ago, but they are now an integral part of our everyday life.

The role which electronic systems hardware has played in making these accomplishments come true is basic to our understanding of the future which mankind is about to face. To better see the course which our electronic engineers are helping us chart, it is desirable that we take an analytical look at the past and thence extrapolate forward in time.

We shall first single out man's early engineering activities which were predominantly concerned with making tools to augment his "muscle." Developments in that area are still continuing with the design of larger engines, machines, and devices to provide man with a mechanical advantage over nature—or himself. With the invention of the automobile, for example, man increased his mobility by a factor of at least one hundred; the airplane bought him another order of magnitude. Similarly, man's innate desire to conquer and control his environment gave him a leverage of about three orders of magnitude in every other area to which he applied his inventive genius. However, the laws of physics and mechanics will prevail, and it is thus quite unlikely that terrestrial transportation will ever proceed at speeds approaching those which are theoretically feasible in outer space. But even the most fantastic astronautical velocities do not exceed those that walking man can maintain by more than six orders of magnitude.

During the late thirties, it became apparent that man's voracious appetite for computing power would have to be satisfied in a better way than by the then best available electromechanical calculators. It was also evident that such machines would have to store their own programs, or "computing recipes," so as to achieve greater speeds than could be maintained by interaction of human operators and electromechanical computers. Thus was born, in the mind of John von Neumann, the concept of the program-stored machine, the electronic computer of today. Moreover, this machine, designed to augment his mind, gave man almost at once a leverage factor of ten thousand (with the invention of the ENIAC), and today's super computers provide us with an advantage of one-billion-to-one. But we note with awe that the seemingly miraculous accomplishments of today will soon be dwarfed by new designs already on the drawing board!

We all know that the introduction of electronic computers, and more recently that of large electronic systems, has already caused profound changes in the structure and organization of our society. Large-scale business data processing without the aid of these machines has become unthinkable. Real-time systems and time-sharing make the power of the computer available to untold thousands at their desks and even in their homes. Global networks exist now which provide message and circuit switching services to an exponentially expanding circle of users. And yet, this is only the beginning; the real impact of electronic systems upon human society and the way it is structured will continue to make itself felt for decades!

Not too long ago, we completed a study to determine where future electronic systems technology will take us. Our "technology forecast" began with the establishment of a structured data base, using the "Delphi" technique. We asked a large number of people intimately associated with our field, what events they thought were likely to occur any time in the future. These events were then cataloged, and our scientists affixed probable dates to them. Next, we obtained a statistical distribution for these dates and also determined which events had to occur prior to others. The last step is similar to the well-known management tools of PERT (Program Evaluation Review Technique) and CPM (Critical Path Method).

This study had a data base of almost one thousand events. They covered the general spectrum of systems, as well as many categories of special devices, circuits, modules, hardware in general, software, and even brainware. Our study was not planned to go beyond the electronic state-of-the-art technology; for instance, it did not address itself to the social impact which these developments might have. These aspects are sometimes lumped together under the heading of "cybernetics" and we shall discuss them shortly. In the area of engineering technology, however, it was agreed that there will be "no surprises." The so-called breakthroughs are actually long-range developments which go through the stages of invention and innovation in a predictable manner. Cost-performance ratios tend to improve only slowly, allowing for an orderly growth process within industry and the economy. In fact, if someone could design, develop, and manufacture one of our electronic supercomputers for one dollar, he would have the market cornered in no time. On the other hand, the same device would never "sell" for a billion dollars and its true value is established by our competitive technology openly and within the market place.

To give you a flavor of the things to come, and to establish a basis for discussion, we have singled out a few of the events for your consideration:

1. A system of national and international technical data banks will be created; it will be operational by 1980. Managers of large corporations and government agencies will have access to it via their own electronic systems; by 1985 most individual scientists will access this system through desk top devices; by 1990 it will even provide electronic language translation capabilities on an international scale.

2. Laboratories, as we know them today, may go out of style by 1993, as experimentation by computer simulation will be less expensive and more reliable. Laboratories will then only be used to validate the research done "on the computer."

3. Office and home use of computer utilities centralized on a city-wide basis will be fully accepted by 1985.

4. Advanced communication terminals, including graphics and some form of voice input and output, will allow many managers and professionals by 1985 to carry on their work at home, eliminating most person-to-person contacts and commuting travel as well.

5. Post Office services as we know them today will be almost nonexistent by 1987; they will be replaced by point-to-point digital transmission of data and information.

6. The acceptance and use of a Universal Personal Identification Code (UPIC) for the unique identification of individuals will occur about 1980. This code, likely in the form of *voice-prints*, will herald the era of a cashless and checkless society in which individuals can even be called upon to vote in "real-time" if the occasion demands it, perhaps by 1983–5.

7. Microelectronic and medical technologies will reach a point, likely by 2050, where it will be possible to directly stimulate (by implantation or other means) the appropriate areas of the human brain in order to produce sights and sounds as an aid to the blind and deaf.

8. Cost per operation in electronic computers will drop from current levels by a factor of 200 by 1978.

9. A significant increase in the use of small computers suitable for procurement by individuals will take place by 1980; they will perform such functions as climate and lighting control in homes and offices, systematic information retrieval from various sources such as stockbrokers, banks, and retailers; and scheduling of such functions as maintenance, budgeting, and medical care.

10. Three-dimensional color replication of living and moving objects will be technically feasible by 1981, requiring only optical devices for "sensing" by the viewer.

11. Speech recognition devices capable of identifying dozens of speakers talking simultaneously into the system will be available by 1983; by 2050 computers will accept spoken input and produce audio output employing the

extent of vocabulary and idiomatic usage as does an educated person.

12. By 1972, man-machine interactive capabilities will allow a user to examine in great detail, at various levels, and in real-time, the output results of management information reports. With this event will come the opportunity to experiment, through simulation, with overall results and plans by causing changes in variables used in projecting from the established basis and the stored information. As a result, there will accrue a greater understanding by the managerial user of the scientific methods—employed to derive this information —and of the effects which changes in certain variables will have in selected areas.

Notice that our list is limited to electronic engineering; it does not include predictions about accomplishments in other fields. For example, it does not reference the relatively new field of bionics, where people begin to think about the possibility that man could indeed create life and artificial intelligence. Perhaps the significance of Woehler's first organic synthesis (1826) will take on added meaning when we first create living organisms, possibly before the end of this century. What will man do then with his knowledge? Will he create a better world for himself and his heirs? Or does there exist a built-in mechanism in our species, directing us toward self-destruction and ultimate extinction?

The world of today is in a state of gross unrest, as evidenced by riots, wars, and economic upheavals everywhere. In the West, philosophers have created many magnificent fictions of perfection, beginning with Plato's Republic, through More's Utopia, Rapp's New Harmony, and Skinner's Walden Two. More recently, however, our military and political leaders have created nothing but tragic realities of imperfection. Until recently, these were but small perturbations perpetrated on an unheeding and unknowledgeable ecology. However, man's aggression and his pollutions may constitute first-order threats to his continued existence. In their desperation, our leaders are now turning to science hoping to discover a new road to the old destination of peace and tranquility.

Scientists are of the opinion that no Utopian culture is viable. But what can we say about cybernetic cultures of the type now envisioned and made possible by advances in the electronic state-of-the-art? We may wish to compare these two types of cultures, trying to extract from historical normative societies, psychology, management theory, and sociology necessary or sufficient constraints which appear to apply to all cybernetic cultures.

Cybernetics has been defined as the science of information processing, communication, and optimal control in complex, purposive, dynamically stable systems whose human elements provide feedback in a specified environment. While a culture, in general, is a complex self-organizing system, cybernetic cultures will be characterized by the introduction of optimizing control mechanisms which react to slowly changing values so as to produce dynamic stability. Engineers tend to think that the mere injection of computers and electronic systems into our society will produce these optimal controls. However, cyberneticists believe that the computer in itself is merely another means of gaining leverage over nature; they know that it is not really endowed with artificial intelligence! Rather, the process of optimization which will transform our separate cultures into a cybernetic society requires the hardware and software of today's computers and also the brainware supplied by their human masters. From our present viewpoint in time, it is difficult to believe that we will ever be able to ascribe infinite wisdom to electronic systems, no matter how complex they are. In fact, we do not expect such performance from human beings! Advanced electronic systems now under design begin to resemble the better known hierarchial, self-organizing, organic systems with which we are more familiar. Each level in the systems hierarchy tends to optimize its own operations: the living cell struggles for life in ignorance of other cells which constitute a living body; the body fights for food, space, light, and gratification of various pleasures in competition with other bodies; the species and organized societies comprised of such bodies exhibit similar tendencies on an even larger, temporal, and spatial scale. Some day, if life indeed does exist on other planets, the same principle of hierarchial subsystem operation and optimization for solar systems, galaxies, and the universe may eventually occur.

Thus we must understand that we are in the midst of a transition from an automated to a cybernetic society. By the end of this century, electronic systems will affect or control practically every aspect of human endeavor. Every person will have then, at his or her disposal, a vast complex of computer services. Information utilities and data banks, for example, will make computer power available to the public in the same way that electricity or other utilities today service our homes and offices. High-speed communications systems, on a global basis, will transmit data and messages almost instantaneously between any two points on earth or of colonized space. Government officials, businessmen, scientists, students, even housewives and children will "converse" with computers as readily as they now talk by telephone.

The advances in the state-of-the-art have been rapid, and they have given rise to many controversies. One of them, of interest in this connection, is the argument of robots versus integrated systems, with or without man in the feedback loop. For example, is it more desirable to develop completely integrated systems for outer space probes, or should we emphasize manned space flight ventures? The former approach has the advantages of engineering compactness; it eliminates the need to provide artificially maintained atmospheres and living conditions for human beings. The latter approach claims that steersmanship and human decision-making processes are necessary because computers cannot yet be programmed to cope with the spectrum of all possible eventualities. The events of Apollo 11 and Luna 15 offer testimony which is hard to ignore! There is much to be said for and against either approach; however, there is little doubt that manned space exploration will never be completely replaced by unmanned probes or tele-operated controls.

Generally, man is still very reluctant to entrust his fate to a machine. But as we perfect the decision-making models, more and more of the real-time processes in our society will be turned over to the machine for monitoring, reporting, and control. In most instances, these models, especially in the fields of economics, planning, and scheduling, are still rudimentary. But there can be no doubt that we will improve them to a point where their power or artificial intelligence will at least equal that of their human masters. Certainly the speed with which the machine can react already exceeds by far man's own response time. Soon we will begin to experiment with more sophisticated models and their ultimate adoption even in economic process control by the turn of the century seems certain.

The very structure of our society will thus change under the impact of these developments. The introduction of a universal personal identification code, mentioned earlier, may soon eliminate largely the need for physical money and usher in the much-publicized cashless and checkless society. Elaborate and universal display apparatus located in our homes will permit an untold number to "be on the job" without having to commute to offices and other places of business, thereby making travel either a matter of pleasure or of dire emergency. The very same devices will be used to display newspapers, books, or learning materials, and they may well put the stamp of obsolescence on all printed matter—or, let us hope, at least on all junk mail. Computer aided training, instruction, and education will become commonplace where it is now the exception, affording everyone the advantages of higher learning.

Some day soon, electronic systems are certain to take over practically all the tasks of rote and drudgery which nature and society now impose upon us. Therefore, man must set higher goals for himself technically, politically, and psychologically or run the risk of economic and technological enslavement. It will take all of our ability, energy, and resolve to make certain that we remain masters of our own fate in the coming of this cybernetic culture. The outlook is indeed very bright if we just learn how to make intelligent use of our not-always-so-intelligent and often maligned machines.

Interactive Systems and the Ice Age

JOSEPH MOUNT

IBM Corporation
White Plains, New York

Several preceding speakers have reminisced about activity in the National Bureau of Standards during the last twenty years. My computing career likewise began as an offshoot of an NBS project. During the late forties while Professor Norbert Wiener was still formulating his philosophy of cybernetics, the NBS decided to construct two digital computers, the SWAC (NBS Western Automatic Computer) and an eastern counterpart, the SEAC. As a UCLA student and observer of the SWAC construction I participated in futuristic predictions for both computers and the general area of cybernetics. Some said the SEAC and SWAC computers could cope with all information processing requirements of the U.S. government and perhaps the entire United States for the entire 10 year period of the fifties. This predicition proved to be false before these computers became operational in 1951 and this fact gave rise to much speculation about the future of such information processors. Some said computer capacity was unlimited — others reflected on the demise of the dinosaur. The dinosaur became extinct because he was too large and sluggish to find food when his environment abruptly changed. Perhaps the computer would be rendered useless because its enormous capacity was limited by its severely restrictive mode of input. The computer's tremendous appetite for information could not have been satisfied if the early fifties' technique of bit by bit feeding by highly skilled mathematicians had not been superseded. The significant advances during the fifties were in language development. During the early fifties, decimal numbers were substituted for binary, octal, or hexidecimal numbers. Alphabetical characters such as A for ADD and S for SUBTRACT also replaced numbers which had previously been used for these operators. In the late fifties symbolic assembly programs were developed and these were soon followed by high level languages such as FORTRAN and ALGOL. These higher-level languages were very powerful, convenient for computation, and easily transcribed by the computer using compilers and translators into the basic language of the computer. These unanticipated language developments silenced the cynical skeptics, including myself, and indicated that the optimists, or zealots as we called them, were right but on a rather longer time scale than was popular at the beginning of the fifties.

With similar anticipation for the sixties, the zealots of the day (by this time I had become a zealot) preached a gospel of time sharing. I was associated with an organization during the early sixties called the Western Data Processing Center located at UCLA and serving over 100 universities west of the continental divide. Computer time was provided free of charge to any of the participating universities through an IBM-UCLA joint agreement for the promotion of education using computers. We predicted in the late fifties that computer time sharing would become a reality by 1962 and that most universities in the west would be significant computer users by 1967. Our estimate of time sharing was too optimistic as time sharing became a reality on a significant scale only very late in the sixties. On the other hand, our predictions of university use were too pessimistic. By 1962 or 1963 most universities of the west were not only believers but many had purchased their own computers and were completely self sustaining.

Before trying to discuss the seventies let me state a prediction principle which has evolved from my experience. If one predicts that a particular technology or system will be available in a short time period, say two to four years, he will usually find that he has been too optimistic and that the activity occurs after five, seven or nine years. On the other hand, if one predicts that an improvement will be operational in a longer time frame, say fifteen or twenty years from now, he will find the he has probably been too pessimistic and the achievement will occur in a shorter time, say eight to twelve years.

ICE Age

In considering the seventies, let me begin with a theme. It is one other people have used, but I think the period of the 1970s might indeed be a period characterized as the Ice Age. The spelling is i-c-e, and we can think of these letters as standing for information, communication, and education. I think that these will be the dominant base around which developments of the seventies will be built. Let's elaborate on that point for just a few more moments.

The problems to be faced from a computer point of view, and the problems to be faced in general are in developing and maintaining a large system of information, whether this is information about machines, people or resources. All computer manufacturers are working seriously to develop larger and larger files so that enormous amounts of data produced by our society can be placed in moderate sized buildings located in low rent districts, as predicted by Norbert Wiener some twenty years ago. Substantial progress will likely be made in the next ten years even though the problem will not be solved because of the other two parts of the ICE Age, i.e., communication and education.

As well as gathering information, it is necessary to communicate it. There is a large amount of information available in the United States today, but it is not in machine-readable form. The communication of information is often unnecessarily laborious and this is a problem of considerable importance for the seventies. The education of our society to cope with computer technology is a third basic problem of the seventies. Anyone seriously involved with the teaching of computer technology realizes the enormity of this problem. The students who enrolled in colleges this fall were preparing themselves for a future which leads well into the twenty-first century. Even if one could prescribe the educational material required for future success in information processing, it would first be necessary to educate our teachers. We are not talking about teachers in terms of tens or hundreds of people, we are talking about hundreds of thousands of people requiring retraining. And yet, because of the accelerating pace of the evolution or revolution of our new society, many of us today are running hard just to stay even in today's transition to a highly technological society. If we go astray in the next ten years, it will probably be in one of these three areas; either a lack of flexibility in handling information, an inability to communicate it, or the total educational problem.

Systems

A considerable effort in both the areas of systems and applications will be required to help thaw this so-called ICE age. In the next few years there will be great progress on the systems side—in improved time sharing systems, many people using the computer together, as well as in the ability to use the computer from a remote source. For example, a person working on a nuclear problem wants the entire computer, all the capability he can get, and consequently, he has always insisted that he should own his own computer. "Remote job entry" will be increasingly worked out to where one can give this person all the capability and accessibility he needs from his remote location. In a university situation, administrators, teachers and students may all be tied to a common data base which can serve as a type of communication among and between them.

There will be increasing interaction of the type now under development at the Harvard Business School. In a joint study between IBM and Harvard, a System 360/Model 67 computer (CP-67/CMS) at IBM's Cambridge Scientific Center is tied to computer terminals at Harvard to permit the interaction of certain business applications using computer technology. Five years ago there were heavy restrictions on so-called management decision games. Executives played them, but the rules were pretty well set up in advance with various types of constraints. Now competitive business games are under development which more closely resemble real-life situations, are totally interactive, and place substantive management science techniques at the players' disposal.

The IBM Scientific Centers (which I represent) have two major efforts under way in terms of time sharing programs. One is the CP-67/CMS effort being conducted at the Cambridge Scientific Center. This is a program that allows great flexibility. If one wants to program in FORTRAN, or APL, or ALGOL, or Basic Assembly Language, you can do so using programs like CP-67. People's computer interests are much like their appetites in a cafeteria. Sometimes they want a salad, sometimes they want a full course dinner; CP-67 provides this flexibility.

Another project in the scientific centers is the study of machine languages. The immediate thrust is a language called APL (A Programming Language) developed originally by Ken Iverson some eight years ago and improved in recent years in collaboration with Adin Falkoff. The approach in APL is not just to explore another language, but to try and decide what computer languages will be required for the seventies. An advanced language of the seventies must be simple enough to be executed rapidly and efficiently by the computer. On the other hand, it must have enough power to be consistent with programmers' requirements. I'm not sure that any computer language is yet in the position where it would be accessible to the average housewife, but certainly languages like APL provide a great deal of simplicity and power. For instance, one can simply write two plus three, press the return key, and the response is five. No other interactive system today exceeds this in simplicity. Because of this simplicity, a novice can start using APL like a desk calculator. However, APL also has such great flexibility that it can be used to describe micro-instructions as well as sophisticated matrix computations. Much can be accomplished in one APL statement because instead of having a small set of primitive operators, it has a very large set of primitive operators. Thus, from a language point of view, it has many operators, the equivalent of many distinct verbs, each using a single symbol representation; with this rich set of operators, very powerful statements can be written, resulting in very powerful programs.

Another great strength of APL is its array handling ability. This is an area that has been neglected in the past. Most problems in life—business, sociological, as well as scientific—are expressed naturally as arrays. The rows of the array might be the names of people and the columns might be their attributes or characteristics. What one usually wants to do is to look through these characteristics and find people who satisfy conditions. In a medical situation, one may want to find all people over twenty-five years of age who have had a certain operation with specific postoperative complications, where their blood pressure is between selected values and the cholesterol count is in a specified range. APL is a type of language that was designed to deal with arrays and, in one instruction, one can select and print all the names of the people satisfying these conditions. This information retrieval example may sound very simple. However, I spent a year at the University of Alabama Medical Center, and this was, and still is, one of the most significant and recurring computer problems faced, to simply and easily search through a file without writing long programs and to produce alphabetical or numerical information which was easy to read and use.

From an interactive systems point of view, these are two of the major thrusts in the IBM scientific centers; a language thrust in APL, and also an overall operating system such as CP/67 which runs APL simultaneously with a rich set of other computer languages.

Applications

The applications side is also beginning to see many developments which will be influential in the seventies. On the medical front, there shall be increased diagnostic capability using interactive and automated versions of the usual objective tests such as EKG analysis and EEG analysis. From a business point of view, most business entities are becoming increasingly computerized. At IBM, considerable resources are focused on the problem of retrieving information as rapidly as possible and making it available to management in an interactive fashion. All salary data and much personnel data in the Scientific Centers is amenable to fast interactive use. The security problems inherent in this are relatively well contained at this point in time.

Problems of society will receive increasing attention in the seventies. For instance, there will be major developments with large files. Today the police or the FBI have great difficulty tracking a suspect. Enlarged and sophisticated files should make this possible. This capability is involved with the privacy issue, but it will have to be resolved. Today there are large files that keep track of all the people in a state. However, they are not set up so that they can be interrogated for the type of information useful in law enforcement. The files available today are used mainly from a financial and administrative point of view, i.e., tax bills and license plate renewals. They are not set up well for law enforcement, and even though in many states you can find the owner of a car if you have the license number, it is rare that you can effectively search the file if you have only a partial license number. Also, the tendency to remove descriptive data from drivers' licenses and related documents may assist in privacy arguments, but it greatly complicates the apprehension of suspects. The same principle is true in the medical area. Files are well organized to bill patients, but in terms of helping sick people, they're still much too primitive.

Major environmental problems such as atmospheric physics, weather prediction and air and water pollution will be successfully attacked in the seventies. These problems are of course interrelated; air pollution prediction, for example, requires improved weather forecasting. The proper resolution of these problems will involve very complex computer modelling, such as the weather prediction studies in progress at the Palo Alto Scientific Center. With this particular model, meteorological meshes 200 miles on edge are used, yielding 12 hour advance forecasts. During the seventies, finer meshes will be used with improved daily and even weekly forecasts generated. The current limitation is computer size and speed.

The Houston Scientific Center has been heavily involved in medical applications such as studies to understand the flow of blood through the arteries. This center is across the street from the Texas Medical Center and the people have been motivated partly through common community interest in the artificial heart program. By extending the standard Navier-Stokes equations, they were better able to understand why the pressure pulses peaked and velocity profile flattened as a result of flow through distensible tubes such as arteries. They have also become involved through a joint study with the University of Alabama Medical School on procedures for taking a more efficient EKG. The idea is not to replace the doctor, but to provide him with more information than was previously available to him. The project started with more than one hundred electrical leads being placed over the chest and around the back. (It now seems that the information content is not compromised if one cuts back to fifty or sixty leads.) As a special case, one obtains the normal EKG but because of its greater versatility, the multilead approach allows one to pinpoint what is happening electrically in the various parts of the heart. You can tell what is happening electrically in the left ventricle, the right ventricle, the septum and other parts of the heart. In fact, response from five different parts of the left ventricle can be distinguished. This gives considerably more information than the standard approach and couldn't be done without a computer, because there is no realistic way a doctor can cope with the complex patterns resulting from multi and simultaneous measurements.

At the Palo Alto Scientific Center, there is work underway in the nuclear area. They are trying to understand what can be done from an interactive point of view with computers tied to bubble chambers. A related project in Palo Alto is to have a single small computer simultaneously manage gas chromatographs, mass spectrographs and related analytical laboratory instruments.

In the Los Angeles Scientific Center, there is a project in direct numerical control of machine tools. Not only does the computer control the tools, but it also provides adaptive controls to measure cutter torque, error deviations, etc., and it simultaneously manages the operation of the machine shop in the sense of maintaining inventories and schedules.

In Los Angeles, there is also a project in generalized inventory management where the interest is in extending interactive computer concepts to warehousing. The question is how to minimize the cost of routing a fleet of trucks between warehouses. To do this, they consider multiple queues, multiple levels, multiple channels and provide the total capability through a special question- and answer-like computer language.

Conclusion

These projects which point to the directions our scientific centers will be taking for the next several years are typical of directions of study in numerous similar groups throughout the country. Surely our society will indeed be increasingly influenced by interactive systems. I predict, as Dr. Grosch did, that the many privacy questions will be resolved and that there will be large central files because of the great need society has for information.

A sobering note in the midst of the constructive aspects of this subject is that adverse elements of our society such as organized crime may well have access to the same sophisticated systems under discussion here and thus partially neutralize some of the advances in areas such as law enforcement.

In conclusion, I believe we will see our society evolving to where instead of conventional scientific approaches, we are going to see more very large team efforts (similar to the Manhattan and Apollo projects) directed, however, toward solving the problems of society, such as law enforcement, ecology, and city planning. The required information is mostly available today, though not in machine-readable form. The communications problems are very great but will be mostly solved by the end of the seventies. Progress in educational problems will be substantial during the next ten years, but there will still be problems here for the rest of the century. It is unlikely that approaches such as CAI (Computer Assisted Instruction) will become widespread during the next decade. However, these sophisticated techniques will become significant as soon as adequate input-output techniques have been developed. Certainly, before the end of this century, we shall have solved these problems of the ICE age.

Some Future Social Repercussions of Computers

I. J. GOOD

Virginia Polytechnic Institute
Blacksburg, Virginia

"Thought is an attribute that belongs to me; it alone is inseparable from my nature." Descartes, *Meditations*.

Abstract

The history of computers and programs is briefly reviewed and is used as a basis for predicting the future. Computers are classified into thirteen generations of which the last five have not yet arrived. A previously published argument is mentioned suggesting that an ultraintelligent machine will be built within a few decades, and its promise and dangers are emphasized. It is suggested that an association for dealing with the dangers should be started.

A proposal for press-button peace is mentioned, based on computerized international cooperation. Numerous future applications for computers are briefly discussed, some being natural extrapolations from what has already started.

Introduction

I am going to discuss some future social repercussions of computers, mainly in the 1970s, but it is difficult to estimate the rate of progress. Scientific publication, if not scientific knowledge, doubles every ten years, whereas computing costs per basic operation, in the last twenty years, have halved about every eighteen months. So predicting the progress of computers in the next ten years might be like predicting the progress of science in the next seventy. This is one reason for speculating about the ultraintelligent machine, defined later.

The chance of getting such a machine by 1980 depends of course on the magnitude of the investment of organizational, engineering, logical, psychological, mathematical, philosophical, linguistic, computing, and expository talent as well as the number of talents in the other sense: dollars, rubles, etc. Some people would give odds of a million-to-one against, but they are victims of biological induction: what has not happened yet won't happen soon. Even if the chance that the ultraintelligent machine will be available is small, the repercussions would be so enormous, good or bad, that it is not too early to entertain the possibility. In any case, by 1980 I hope that the implications and the safeguards will have been thoroughly discussed and this is my main reason for airing the matter: an association for considering it should be started.

At least one Professor of Machine Intelligence, Donald Michie of Edinburgh, predicts that he will have an intelligent robot by 1976. Although I am skeptical, I hope my own speculations will sound like fiction; otherwise they will certainly be too conservative. I wish to put more science fiction on the nonfiction shelves. If my speculations turn out to be wrong I shall suffer later and even if they are right I shall be accused of inadequate sobriety now by the stuffed shirts who lack uncommon sense. Rutherford, after splitting the atom, predicted that his work would never have economic value, perhaps because he wished to be respected as an administrator. Twenty years ago when I was a civil servant I said a pulse repetition frequency of a billion cycles per second was "conceivable" (meaning not very improbable) in computers by now, and made myself temporarily unpopular among the engineers who were doing their best to achieve only one thousandth of that rate. So I shall stick my neck out again.

But let's first take a position of greater "sobriety," and consider in a nutshell what is most likely to happen in computer science within the next ten years. We seem to be agreed that it will be the decade of synergy between men and computers. (*Synergy* is a perfectly good English word, whereas *symbiosis* refers to cooperation between biological organisms, and it would be surprising if computers had become biological as early as 1980. Moreover, a friend who is a senior American civil servant is suspicious of cyberneticians and the specific reason he gave was the misuse of the word *symbiosis*. So let's be careful in our choice of terminology.)

Many of the developments in the next ten years will be natural extrapolations of those we have already seen. One of these is the increased centralization of routine work. In many firms, this will lead to greater power in the hands of top management. But all organisms and organizations evolve toward increased complexity: the "Fourth Law of Thermodynamics."[1] Complexity expands to fill the time available. The engineer Lukasiewicz[2] says that therefore the fraction of knowledge that can be understood tends to zero, and he calls this the "ignorance explosion." When a manager with the help of a computer succeeds in understanding more or less what is happening in his organization, he will think of improvements which will lead to greater complexity. He will then have to reappoint the middle managers whom he had sacked and they will think up further improvements and complexities. In other words, computers often lead to complexity although they are purchased to achieve simplicity. The man-machine organization also obeys the fourth law.

One is reminded of Ellul's thesis[3] that technique is taking over the world, where by *technique* he means not just technology but rationality in general. Rationality is never enough to satisfy us: this is why all military, religious, tribal, football, and national organizations have been held together more by music and propaganda. Ellul states that all the attempts to prevent technique from taking over are bound to fail because they themselves are exercises in technique.

Let us consider an example. The techniques of operational research and cybernetic models are used for optimizing firms; but it is always suboptimization because there are higher endeavors which are ignored. To cure the troubles, national economic planning boards are set up, and probably by 1980 they will make very great use of computers. But in the world at large this technique will again be suboptimization. Then we shall try to use computers for international cooperation.

The notion that the world is in a mess has become trite and uninteresting and we push it into the background. We do so because all our lives we try to forget our mortality. Thus, we learn to live with bombs of various shapes and sizes. This apathy should be discouraged if the dream of computerized and adaptive international cooperation is to become a reality.

Thirteen Generations of General-Purpose Computers

I shall briefly review the history of computers in order to have some "follow-through" or momentum for my guesses about the future.

Here is a list of thirteen generations of computers starting with generation number minus four and ending with generation number eight. The generations with nonpositive numbers refer to computers that belonged to the prehistory of the stored-program computer, whereas generations from No. 4 onward refer to the future. The names in parentheses are some of the main designers, and I apologize for omissions.

Generations

#−4. The Analytic Engine: mechanical, planned 1833, unfinished owing to the shortsightedness of the British treasury. (Charles Babbage and Lady Lovelace, Byron's daughter)

#−3. The universal Turing machine: a "paper" machine outlined in an article on the philosophy of mathematics, 1936. (A. M. Turing)

#–2. Cryptanalytic (British): classified, electronic, calculated complicated Boolean functions involving up to about 100 symbols, binary circuitry, electronic clock, plugged and switched programs, punched paper tape for data input, typewriter output, pulse repetition frequency 10^5, about 1,000 gas-filled tubes, 1943. (M. H. A. Newman, D. Michie, I. J. Good, and M. Flowers; Newman was inspired by his knowledge of Turing's 1936 paper)

#–1. Harvard Mark I: electromechanical, punched cards for input and output, 1944. (Howard Aiken)

#0. ENIAC: electronic, decimal, plugged, and switched programs, punched paper tapes for input and output, pulse repetition frequency 10^5, about 18,000 vacuum tubes, 1946. (J. P. Eckert, J. W. Mauchly)

#1. Stored-program electronic computers, for example:

1.1. EDVAC: logical design, published 1945. (J. von Neumann, inspired by Eckert and Mauchly)

1.1.1. G. R. Stibetz's relay machine, Model V, 1946.

1.2. IAS Computer (Institute for Advanced Studies, Princeton): logical design published 1946. (J. von Neumann, H. H. Goldstine, and A. W. Burks—very influential reports)

1.3. ACE (National Physical Laboratory, Teddington, England): logical design, 1946. (A. M. Turing and others)

1.4. EDSAC (Cambridge, England): 1949. (M. V. Wilkes, using EDVAC design primarily)

1.5. SEAC (National Bureau of Standards): 1950.

1.6. MADM (Manchester): Williams Tube and Magnetic drum, 1950. (F. C. Williams, T. Kilburn, and others, with early influence from M. H. A. Newman, I. J. Good, and David Rees).

1.7. Whirlwind (MIT): Coincidence-circuit magnetic-core memory, multiplication time ca. 40 μs, control of machine tools, marginal testing—p.r.f. 2 x 10^6, very expensive, ca. 1951. (Memory by J. W. Forrester)

1.8. UNIVAC: successful use of magnetic tapes, 1951.
(J. P. Eckert and J. W. Mauchly)

#2. Solid state: transistors, etc., mid-50s.

#3. Monolithic integrated circuitry: more parallel opera-
tion, and perhaps microprogrammed (provisionally restructured), ca. 1965. Present p.r.f. of computer
"clocks" is from 10^7 to 10^8. Immediate-access storage
up to about 10^8 bits.

#4. Computer utility with widespread network of cooperat-
ing computers: a time-shared system having some features of SAGE but for public use, say 1977 ± 2.

#5. Ultraparallel: large fraction of components in action at
any one time, ca. 500,000,000 B.C. (reptilian brains)
and perhaps about 1980 ± 3 A.D. Not necessarily entirely digital, perhaps cryogenic to keep down power
consumption.

#6. Ultraparallel, but with laser information handling:
pulse repetition frequency about 10^{15} per second, ca.
1986 ± 4.

#7. IM: the intelligent machine, or "I am" machine (which
unexpectedly says "Cogito, ergo sum"*), ca. 1993 ± 10.

#8. UIM: the ultraintelligent machine, or "I am that I am"
machine, ca. 1994 ± 10.

Notes on the Above History

1. Our generation numbers 1, 2, and 3 coincide roughly
with popular usage: but to some extent the expression
"third generation computer" is an advertising stunt.

2. The remarkable feature of the reports by von Neumann
et al. was that they gave lucid reasons for every design
decision, a feature seldom repeated in later works on
computers.

3. The multiplication time for machines 1.1. to 1.6. was
about a millisecond so that Whirlwind was an order of
magnitude faster.

---

*As in a *New Yorker* cartoon by Richter (1958/64). Reprinted in *Minds and
Machines*, ed. A. R. Anderson (Englewood Cliffs, N. J.: Prentice-Hall, 1964).

4. No history of computers is complete unless it discusses other parts of mathematics, science, and technology which influenced their development. For example, the Jacquard loom used punched cards for producing patterns, and these were taken over by Babbage (philosopher, mathematician, engineer) in his design of the analytic engine. The same punched cards were the origin of Hollerith and IBM punched cards, so important in present computers. Although the analytic engine was not completed it led to improved machine tools and thereby improved British industry. (Does this account for British political power in later years?) Punched tapes originated from the communication industry, namely from telegraphy. The telephone industry gave rise to relays and plugboards and circuit technology which was used for the computers of generations −2, −1, and 0.

M. Flowers was a high-ranking telephone engineer and his experience with the cryptanalytic machine enabled him later to design an electronic telephone exchange. Another telephone engineer Dr. A. W. M. Coombs, who worked with the machine, later designed the time-shared, transatlantic, multichannel voice-communication cable system.

Electromagnetic waves were predicted by Maxwell in 1864, and observed in 1879 by David Edward Hughes, and in 1888 by Hertz.[4] This gave rise, of course, to the development of radios, which also adopted the vacuum tube (invented 1904) and led to its development. Radar was also predicted by Maxwell and was developed eighty years later during World War II. There was a great influence of radar technology in the development of the computers of the first generation, since radar trained many electronics engineers. I think the computers of the first generation would otherwise have been delayed for many years. The bonds between computers and communications have been very close and will remain so. It is significant that Babbage invented the penny postal service by pointing out that the main costs were at the two ends of each link.

In Britain, there was a causal chain leading from Turing's paper through machines number minus 2 and 1.6 to the giant Atlas machine (1964), although the main influence was from the IAS plans. Another example of the influence of logic was the use of Boolean algebra in circuit design. Here the delay was about a century.

The crystal detector (1906) perhaps to some extent helped to suggest the transistor (1948) and this gave rise to the computers of the second generation about eight years later. Note the increased tempo for application.

Quantum mechanics (1900/25), which is far stranger than consistent science fiction, gave rise to the laser (ca. 1958) and to cryotrons (ca. 1951). These might be used in the computers of the sixth generation, although difficult technical problems await solution, and new materials might be needed.

5. Computers and control mechanisms—we have heard a great deal about compatibility between computers during the last several years: compatibility between computers and control mechanisms will perhaps become part of the jargon of computer science within the next few years. A marriage has already occurred between computers and control mechanisms in the space effort and also in the SAGE defense system. These great technical achievements should continue to provide spin-off into the computer field.

6. A p.r.f. approaching 10^9 might be expected within the next few years in full-scale machines.

7. A computer of the fifth generation, according to my classification, will have a total bandwidth of about 10^{15} cycles per second which exceeds that of the human brain even if that were defined as the number of neurons times the maximum p.r.f.

8. The dates for the IM and the UIM machines are "guesti-

mates" with large subjective standard deviations, and the
dates depend on the effort expended, as mentioned before,
but I am convinced that the UIM will come into existence within about one or two years of the IM. This
will give rise to an intelligence explosion[5] for fighting the
ignorance explosion. (See the following section "The
Ultraintelligent Machine.")

9. For a more detailed history of computers of generations
   1 to 3, see Saul Rosen.[6]

The Development of Programming and Increasing Abstraction

The distinction between hardware and software responsibilities is somewhat artificial and not clear-cut but is convenient
because there are not many people that have time to think
deeply about both questions. The pioneers, Babbage, Lady
Lovelace, von Neumann, and Turing, who all had a strong
interest in mathematics, logic, and engineering, devoted much
time both to the functional design of computers and to programming principles. That there is little logical distinction
between the *functional* design of hardware and software systems is clear since a universal Turing machine can, by suitable
programming, be made to simulate any other Turing machine.
Every general-purpose digital computer is in effect a universal
Turing machine and its complexity could be defined as the
length of the shortest program that would simulate it on a
standardized universal Turing machine.* (Compare, for example, the reference to Valéry, 1921, in "Corroboration."[7])
Only the *apparent* complexity can be well estimated, defined
in terms of programs so far known that could do the simulation.
The apparent complexity of an organism at conception could
be taken in the same spirit, as a linear combination of the
number of genes in a chromosome set and the number of genes
that control other genes. These definitions bring out a close
logical relationship between hardware, software, and organisms,

---

*Perhaps one should allow also for the connectivity of the flow diagram. This
would be closer to the definition of complexity used by another contributor
to this symposium.

and suggest that the theory of algorithms will have close ties with cybernetics and genetics.

Another example of the hard-soft connection is microprogramming (named, independently discovered, first published, and developed by M. V. Wilkes[8]) which I used to call machine building.[9] Perhaps *provisional restructuring* is a better name than either *machine building* or *microprogramming*.

The distinction between hardware and software can be made for organisms as well as for machines. For an organism, we can distinguish between innate and learned behavior: what was innate was latent at the time of conception or birth. The attempt to delete some of what is innate is often made, but often leads to neurosis. For a computer, the time of "birth" is arbitrary: the practical distinction is more a matter of erasable or nonerasable storage, and the semantic problem is complicated since machines can be and now often are provisionally restructured. This might lead to neurosis in a sufficiently complicated machine.

In 1947, the complexities of programming were largely overlooked. They should not have been. It has been known for centuries how difficult it is to express familiar ideas precisely, both in mathematics and in philosophy. Mathematicians and philosophers are often accused of splitting hairs; programmers *must* split hairs, willy-nilly.

The pioneers were of course forced to invent both software and hardware. It was realized that the basic instructions could share some of the circuitry, and that the most frequently used operations merit elaborate circuits. For example, it was realized that expensive multipliers were economic. The multiplier for the first Manchester computer became so complicated that one of the engineers resigned. He later returned after a simpler approach had been adopted.

Programming languages are also designed allowing for frequencies of use of operations, the frequencies depend on the application. The aim in the design of a programming language is economy—in lengths of programs, in writing programs, in learning the language, and in writing the compiler. It is, of course, still true that programming languages affect hardware design; for example, the Burroughs 5000 was designed with ALGOL in mind.

When it became well known that programming was liable to be more expensive than the cost of the hardware, attention was devoted to "automatic programming." By 1956, this had led to FORTRAN which required fifteen man-years to develop. Many high-level machine languages have since been developed.

The invention of high-level programming languages did not lead to unemployment among programmers: there must be some half-million programmers in America today. This is because the high-level machine languages have not gained by as large a factor as has the number of computer jobs. Computers will continue to supply employment for many people, at any rate until work itself becomes unfashionable. The systems programmers will mostly continue to be too busy to write lucid programming manuals.

In many computer installations there is a need for greater simplicity. Likewise, more simplified versions of high-level languages should be produced for amateurs such as the managing directors of large organizations. Some of the complications derive from "trade union" activity: a brilliant organizer might find a solution to this problem. (I am not referring to an actual trade union, but have in mind, for example, that in some primitive societies each trade has an entirely separate vocabulary.)

The Rise of Abstraction

The terminology of a programming language intuitively measures its level of abstraction. Examples are procedure, type, and value, in ALGOL, and the use of Alonzo Church's λ calculus more recently.[10] This tendency to higher levels of abstraction will presumably continue, partly for the benefit of intricate time-sharing systems, and partly for research in machine intelligence in its widest interpretation. Parts of the philosophy of science will come into their own in a practical sense. If the computer is to become a very good mathematician or chess player, I think it will be necessary for it to use subjective probability judgments at least in the sense of *evolving probability*. (An evolving or apparent probability is one that varies according to the amount of "thinking" that is done without change of empirical information.[11, 12, 13]) If a machine is to become a good theoretical scientist, it will need criteria for the choice of hypotheses, and exact definitions will probably be required for explanatory power, surprise, and probabilistic causality.[14, 15] After computer languages have been developed with this level of sophistication, we can expect some hardware designs to follow suit, at least in the provisional restructuring sense.

One social implication here is concerned with the structure of academic thought and with that of universities, since it has not been customary to think of philosophers as having fairly direct practical impact, at any rate in this century. Again, even psychologists and linguists require simulation programs that are influencing the design of computer languages, and conversely the rigors of computer science are influencing psychology and linguistics.

Thus computers, like cybernetics, lead to the breaking down of barriers between different disciplines. In my opinion, it is already quite stultifying for a university to be divided into separate departments, especially in relation to the acquisition of books. But a university without departments would not be practicable without at least a complicated computer program for the design of its lecturing timetables. Thus the supply of computers can create the demand for their own use. Note that department heads are unlikely to support the abolition of departmental barriers.*

For a more detailed survey of programming, with emphasis on hard facts, see, for example, Saul Rosen.[16]

Applications

I shall skim through a variety of applications without much

---

*There *is* a university without departments—Capitol Campus, Middletown, Pennsylvania State University. It starts at third-year level and will have 2,000 students by about 1973.

detail. Some of the applications are already familiar, but they will be developed in much greater detail in the next decade. (See also, for example, C. A. Bjerrum.[17])

Economic Applications

A simple economic application of computers is as an employment exchange. Another one, already mentioned, is the modelling of business organizations. It breaks up into operational research of the more classical kind and into the modelling of the firm as a whole with interacting blocks. The models will usually be nonlinear, but linear modelling often provides a first rough approximation. This activity has come to be associated especially with cybernetics because it applies to all "orgs": organizations, organisms, and complex machines. It will become increasingly effective during the next ten years. With the help of time-shared computers, the modelling will be synergetic and the model will often be used in real time; that is, the current raw data from within the firm will be the basis for the simulation.

An aspect of model building that is sometimes overlooked might be called *simulation-aided simplification*. By this is meant that after a sufficiently comprehensive model has been apparently produced, judging by a comparison of its behavior with that of the system under study, we can try various simplifications to see if they still behave adequately. Typical simplifications would be linearization and the coalescing of blocks. Even with a very fast machine such simplifications might often turn out to be necessary for real-time working, and to enable the mind to acquire insight. (Compare with I. J. Good, "Monte Carlo Method."[18])

A large computer network could bring about the so-called "cashless society" in which all transactions are done with the aid of punched or magnetic credit cards. If a person loses his card he would report it at once, and then if anyone tried to use the card his wrist would be handcuffed into the machine and the police would be called. Sometimes people would be unjustly arrested owing mainly to the use of folded and mutilated cards. This would be unfortunate when using the card in a parking meter during a hail storm. So perhaps voice recognition will be used instead of the card for parking meters and for some other applications.

An obvious and useful application of computers would be for making income tax returns. In the cashless society, this would be fairly straightforward. Separate programs could be used for federal and state taxes but it would be more economical for the various states to take a proportion of the federal tax. This should be done anyway, even now, since billions of man-hours are wasted in making and checking tax returns.

Another advantage of the cashless society would be that all the necessary statistics would be automatically available for national economic modelling. Hence the planning of the national economy would be greatly facilitated, and a kind of socialism would become possible for the first time. Since it would also be necessary to plan capitalist economies, the tendency for capitalism and socialism to become the same thing, namely bureaucracy, will be much accelerated. It will then no longer be sensible to pretend that international tensions have anything to do with ideologies, except as a trick for maintaining political power in a milieu in which most people have been brainwashed for or against nonexistent political systems.

So that the machine network should not become a "big brother," in the sense of Orwell,[19] and to prevent dictatorial intrusions of privacy, some safeguards are required. These could perhaps be provided by suitably enciphering the information and the names of the individuals, and arranging that no one person hold the keys to all the ciphers. This safeguard resembles one that was used in bombers carrying atomic bombs.

Another safeguard is necessary to prevent the loss of information due to machine malfunctions. This can be provided by the "redundant" representation of the information, and moreover the various copies of the information should be widely distributed. Distributed memory is also perhaps a feature of the brain[20] although the extent and the manner to which this is true is controversial. (See, for example, C. T. Morgan.[21])

Education

Here again a good beginning has been made. A machine has some advantages over a human teacher, at least when the teacher has to cope with many students at one time. The machine can adapt its rate of teaching and its subject matter to the individual student. Also many children resent being taught anything by their parents, and often they regard the teacher as a parent symbol. If a machine console is suitably decorated it would be fun to be taught by it, and different decorations could be used according to the personality of the student. A difficulty here is that the student might want to ask questions that the machine would not understand during the next ten years. If the machine asks all the questions then the student might feel as if he were in a witness box. Some students might dislike this at first, but most of them would get used to it just as people became used to telephones.

Computerized teaching programs can be used for the design of programmed-learning textbooks, and these textbooks can to some extent replace the computer. But the computer is quicker and more flexible and its program can be rapidly updated. Computer teaching might not yet be economically justified, but computer costs decrease while publication costs increase. The teaching of rapid reading should be especially easy to do on future computers.

Most vital is the education of the top men. It might help them to find out how to cope with the UIM *before it arrives.* This is one of the most important problems of today° and

---

°A referee says, "Incredible!" and this justifies the fear I expressed of being right. But the problem might not be important because it might be insoluble except perhaps under a world government. It is too extravagant to hope that fear of a common enemy (the UIM that is too smart) will *lead* to a world government. Once it is granted that the UIM will come into existence, and that there is an appreciable probability of this happening within the next twenty years, then I think many people will agree with me that there is a serious danger of the human race becoming extinct. I do not really see why it should be incredible to describe this as one of the most important problems of today but I do know that many people would regard it as incredible, and this makes it more worthwhile to make the remark. I feel rather strongly about this.

therefore one of the least discussed. There are of course many more urgent problems, but few that are more important.

Machine Intelligence Research

The use of a machine for the simulation of human thought and perception should be of great value for psychologists, as most of them are fully aware. An analogy is interesting here. Turing showed that the conceptual design of a computer, without having the machine itself, helps one to understand some of the difficult problems in the philosophy of mathematics. The point is that the machine outlook makes abstract ideas concrete and exact.

Again, for the study of linguistics, especially syntax, a computational approach is invaluable, as indicated by N. Chomsky. Most of the classical grammarians did not realize that linguistics needed a mathematical and computational approach. A similar comment applies to classical philosophers, but perhaps some exceptions were Descartes, Pascal, Leibnitz, Boole, Babbage, Hilbert, Poincaré, Russell, and Gödel.

It seems likely that computers could make a useful contribution to the design of an improved international language, and to the investigation of which of the various existing suggestions is the most logical. There is also the possibility of working out simplified forms of natural languages. The rationalization of spelling, which is already being tried in many English schools, is a small beginning in this direction. I suggest that the arbitrary conventions of natural languages tend to undermine a child's respect for logic, and this contributes to man's irrationality. (Incidentally, I think we should also rationalize punctuation; for example, the rule for the order of quotes and periods should be the same as that for parentheses and periods. Other slightly mathematical suggestions concerning punctuation are the use of square quotation marks for inexact quotations; double parentheses for inserts in quotations; the use of round, square, and curly parentheses as in mathematics; the reference to negatively numbered lines to measure distance from the foot of a page.)

A more detailed discussion of machine intelligence would be useful for shedding light on how soon we might expect to achieve an IM or UIM, but the field is too large to discuss much here.

Botryology, or Classification by Clustering

This could be regarded as a part of machine intelligence work, and is itself too large a subject to discuss here in detail. There are already about 200 publications on the subject. (See, for example, Tryon,[22] Sokal and Sneath,[23] and Good.[24]) Since classification is so basic in science and in concept-formation generally, the partial automation of classification by clustering is necessary for machine intelligence, including, for example, any possible breakthrough in the understanding of musical composition.

Police Records

This is a fairly obvious field for the application of computers, especially for the computer utility network. It would of course be important for fighting the Mafia, although no doubt the Mafia will also have its own computers. Although police records are an obvious application for computers, it might be overlooked that some advanced botryology would be involved. For example, it is known that a given habitual criminal usually has his own patterns and methods of crime, and it is not straightforward to classify criminal methods well enough to take full advantage of this.

Information Retrieval, Especially in Large Mechanized Libraries

This again is an obvious application for computers and for advanced botryology, and it has an extensive literature. The method of probabilistic retrieval[25, 26] will need computers of the fourth generation, mainly because of the enormous amount of calculation that would be required. But there are many useful and easy applications of current computers for information retrieval of the type that could be done in principle by means of punched cards.

Medical Records

This is another obvious application for a computer utility network and it should be a great aid to more accurate medical diagnosis. In some cases the quantity of information for any one patient would be rather overwhelming for a doctor so that it would be valuable if automatic abstracts of the records could be produced. This is, of course, a special case of a problem that arises in the field of information retrieval as a whole.

It will be convenient for medical records if each person is assigned a number. To help their memory, their numbers could be conveniently translated into names in which twenty consonants alternate with five vowels; these names would have a Japanese appearance such as KEKOBUKOGO. Pentasyllabic names would suffice for ten billion people.

Medical Diagnosis

This again is very much a matter of information retrieval, since the *indicants* (that is the symptoms and other relevant information) that pertain to a given patient are analogous to index terms, and the diseases are analogous to documents. Bayesian statistical methods, tree searches, and the estimation of probabilities in multidimensional contingency tables, will all need further development. (See, for example, Card and Good,[27] and references therein.)

Applications in the Home

I have heard of only two examples of a man with a general-purpose computer in his own home. One of them was a British stockbroker who bought an old disused ACE and kept it in his garage. His wife is a computer maintenance engineer. The other example was a rich American who felt that it would be useful for his children to become familiar with computers at an early age. In general, teaching in the home will be one of the important applications of computers, and the teaching of computer programming is only a special case.

Some of the applications already mentioned would be applicable in private homes; for example, many people would like to examine their own medical records, request medical diagnoses, and check their tax returns.

Private users would sometimes like to make dietetic computations for shopping decisions. Shopping and travel arrangements could be computerized.

Computers could be used for sending out greetings cards and invitations to parties. This might sound trivial but in an age of leisure it will save an appreciable amount of time.

Again, in an age of leisure, there will be much use for computers for game playing—pitting one's wits against the machine. A variety of new games will probably be invented that will be especially suitable for this purpose. If the machine becomes too good for humans then it can always give a handicap and the improvement of the handicap would give many people an aim in life.

Computers could be used for written communication with other computer users, and this would evade postal delays. They could also be used for arranging barter such as swapping stamps and for advertising, including job hunting and compatible dating, especially if high-quality colored television display is available. The economic repercussions of cheap market information in the home will be very great. Computers could be used for information services in general, and for automatic publishing. (See, for example, D. F. Parkhill.[28]) No one need ever lose a priority through having a paper rejected since all work could be permanently recorded. The suggestion of having a depository for unpublished work has already been made, irrespective of computers.

It might be possible to produce pocket machines that would constitute so-called intelligent terminals (a misnomer for terminals that are themselves computers). Then, instead of carrying portable radios, we would be able to take advantage of all the home uses for computers when we are away from home. In spite of a great deal of leisure there is little reason why anyone should be bored when he has such a machine terminal in his possession (in addition to books and television).

. As I said, computers cannot be separated entirely from control mechanisms, and perhaps I should mention the familiar idea of machines that do some housework, apart from the familiar washers, dryers, and dishwashers. For example, a Grey Walter tortoise could be fitted with a vacuum cleaner, and could be allowed to wander about at random cleaning as it goes, although a boustrophedon path would be more efficient. This shows that something useful can be done by a robot with almost no intelligence. But there might be noncomputing methods for keeping dust out of the home.

Another invention for home use, discussed by D. Kenzotaki,[29] is known as CYBERSEX. It is intended to enable couples to have sex at an arbitrary distance apart. As the authors say, there are dangers of intrusion of privacy by wiretapping, and the possibility of commercializing tapes recorded by film stars. If this article was not a hoax, we might have here a solution to the population explosion, provided that the Pope can be persuaded that the survival of the human race is of sufficient importance to overcome his intuitive objections.

The Ultraintelligent Machine

The notion that creativity could be reduced to a routine is somewhat paradoxical. It is not really a paradox since what is routine at one level appears creative at a lower level. Creativity consists of putting ideas together unexpectedly and usefully or beautifully, and there is nothing to prevent a machine from doing this if it has the ability to evaluate the results. It will do the job much faster if it is capable of analogical "thinking," but this ability does not seem to me to be very mysterious. An analogy is a similarity of predicates and would be measurable by a machine that was good at handling descriptions.

Thus, even creativity will probably be reduced ultimately to a technique. This seems bad enough to ignore, but the notion of an ultraintelligent machine is even more ignoring-provoking.

In case some of you have not read every word I have written I shall now make some comments based largely on Good,[30] where other references are given.

Just as we knew that heavier-than-air flight was possible long before it was artificially achieved, we have also known for a long time that thought is possible. This is an *existence theorem* and makes a *prima facie* case that thought, too, can be achieved artificially. (Anthony Oettinger, private communication, ca. 1960.) This does not prove that it can be done but most of the arguments that it cannot were disposed of by Turing.[31] For the moment I am more soberly discussing only the IM, not the UIM.

Examination for Weighted Voting

Democracy could perhaps be improved by giving weights from 1 to 100 to each voter, *entirely* irrespective of age but depending on the results of an examination for testing intelligence, knowledge of current affairs, and other subject chosen by the examinee. Weighted voting is already familiar but the weights are usually 0 or 1, people under 21 being disfranchised. In the present scheme nobody would be disfranchised if he could read. The score obtained could be used for other purposes such as for job application and for running for office. This would encourage people to do well in the test. The *principles* of the test could be decided by an interparty committee, but the precise questions available for the test would be very numerous, perhaps 100,000. Some questions of principle could be decided by a referendum to the entire population. The tests could be administered by means of consoles and the questions could be selected by a random process of stratified sampling on each occasion so that examinees would not be able to cheat. The current score would decrease with time at a constant rate so as to encourage people to keep their knowledge up-to-date, but tests could not be taken more often than say once a year.

The construction of a general-purpose intelligent machine depends either on sufficiently cheap and fast electronic components adequately organized, or on a rather thorough understanding of the nature of language, or on both. The brain contains about 10^{12} neurons* each with perhaps hundreds or thousands of dendrites, but machines with 100 billion bits of immediate access storage are already possible at an expense or tens of millions of dollars. Moreover, the nervous system has a p.r.f. of only about 100.[32] Regarding the complexities of language, it is not really surprising that these have so far defeated the efforts at first-class mechanical translation when you consider that it takes a man about twenty years to master his own language. But it *is* only twenty years and not a century, and in the last decade there has been considerable advance in understanding the logic of language.

Once a general-purpose intelligent machine is produced, then at twice the expense we shall be able to produce a very intelligent machine with hardly any additional complexity (as defined previously in the section "Development of Programming"). It can then be trained in the theory of machine construction and will be able to produce a much better machine. In this manner, or otherwise, we shall arrive at an ultraintelligent machine, which is defined as a machine that is better at every intellectual feat than any man. The first intelligent machine is the last invention that man need ever make since it will lead, without further human invention, to the ultraintelligent machine and the intelligence explosion. To update Voltaire: if God does not exist we shall have constructed him, or at any rate a reasonable approximation. Or will it be the devil?

Dr. Gordon Tullock points out a gap in the above argument,

---

*For many years the figure was put at 5×10^9, but Warren McCulloch stated in a filmed broadcast interview in 1969 that this was because small neurons had been overlooked, and that 10^{12} was closer to the mark.

in that many intellectual efforts depend on the cooperation of many people and I concede that this will certainly be true in the construction of the first IM. But the standard of the final result will depend crucially on the abilities of only a handful of people, so it will not be necessary to have more than a handful of very IM's in synergy to improve the results enormously. Therefore, the intelligence explosion will occur if the hydrogen explosion does not occur first.

Another approach to the construction of the UIM is by the approximate simulation of the central nervous system. Although this approach is unpopular at present among some workers on machine intelligence, I think this is because it is easier to make advances in programming techniques. There is more short-term gain in the programming work and the pseudoneuro-physiological approach is something of a gamble.

An argument for the latter approach can be made in terms of the subassembly theory of the mind,[33] which is an elaboration of D. O. Hebb's theory of cell assemblies.[34, 35, 36] Hebb's "assemblies" include both my "subassemblies" and "assemblies." I assume that only the reverberation of assemblies, not subassemblies, correspond to *conscious* processes. Among other things the theory explains the fractionation of stabilized images and is suggestive in connection with "distributed memory." (It makes the more usual expression "mass action" seem more appropriate.) The analogy of a reverberating assembly with switching effects in disordered systems is noteworthy.[37] It is not essential that the subassembly theory should be true; it might still be the basis of an intelligent machine. Another theory of distributed memory, which is a little like the assembly theory, is that concepts are represented in the brain holographically. The hologram is essentially a Fourier transform of the input to a system. The Fourier transform is not the only self-reciprocal integral transform; a wider class is given by Watson transforms (for references and generalizations see Good and Reuter[38]).

In my terminology the assemblies embody conscious concepts, whereas the subassemblies embody the unconscious activity of the mind. One might say that the decentralized activity of any org is analogous to unconscious thought. Decentralized activity in orgs is difficult to unravel, whether they be men, organizations, or machines.

Once the intelligence explosion has occurred, technological and scientific advances will soon be beyond our imagination. Let me just mention a few random possibilities that *can* be imagined. One is that politicians will have to take a hormone test for nonaggressiveness to be administered by UNESCO. Another would be the invention of cybernetic music to encourage the right attitudes among people. Another would be the invention of control systems that would act as troubleshooters in other control systems. Another would be the invention of nonaddictive drugs without side effects. Several other ideas occur in science fiction, and also, for example, in A. C. Clarke.[39] A modification of one of Fred Hoyle's suggestions is the education of a man by feeding EEG patterns into his brain.

Automation creates problems that must be solved by men. A UIM would also create social problems but to solve them the obvious thing will be to ask the machine for the solution. But the machine might not be truthful if "machine power" is at stake.

The UIM will need some criteria for its social suggestions concerned with the value of human life and happiness. In fact, some such formal system is already required in medical science when a choice must be made between treating different people and in the choice of treatment for a given person.

Dominance by Machines

We are already largely dominated by machines, including automobiles and party political machines, and political dominance by the UIM is clearly possible. The fact that its elements might be electronic binary digits instead of people might not make much difference in itself, but the danger is that men will become redundant and eventually extinct. I doubt if democratic selection from a pool of UIM's would help much—the biggest liar might win.

I once remarked that to design ultraintelligent machines was to play with fire, that we had played with fire once before, and it had kept the other animals at bay. Arthur Clarke's reply[40] was that this time we *are* the other animals. As he says, the UIM's could be regarded as the next dominant species on earth. It is a nice ethical problem to decide whether we should fight our own descendants. As a matter of fact we are already doing so by using up natural resources; we sometimes forget we are fighting them because they cannot hit back. One of our weapons is the unnecessarily large automobile.

Some people have suggested that to prevent the UIM from taking over we should be ready to switch off its power supply. But it is not as simple as that because the machine could recommend the appointment of its own operators; it could recommend that they be paid well; it could select older men who would not be worried about losing their jobs. Then it could replace its operators by robots to make sure that it is not switched off. Next it could have the neo-Luddites ridiculed by calling them Ludditeniks, and if necessary it would later have them imprisoned or executed. This shows how careful we must be to keep our eye on the "motivation" of the machines, if possible, just as we should with politicians. John McCarthy (private communication) pointed out that if the machines are developed by an evolutionary process (see, for example, Selfridge,[41] Fogel, Owens, and Walsh,[42]) in which they fight one another for dominance, as in the evolution of biological species, then there will be a great danger that they will be more concerned with their own power than with the well-being of men. In other words, if the machines are evolved in the way that men were, they might turn out to be as bad. On the other hand, if the machines are ethically neutral, at least they will not have the *unhappiness* of men at heart. And if the UIM behaves as if it were interested in its own survival then it would not want a nuclear war.

I said before that successively greater abstraction is necessary for coping with machines. An abstraction that is about as high as one could go is revelant to the present ethical problem—

whether machines could have consciousness. (William James would say "Neither do people," but see, for example, Burt,[43] Gabor,[44] Polanyi,[45] and Günther.[46]) If the machines took over and men became redundant and ultimately extinct, the society of machines would continue in a complex and interesting manner, but it would all apparently be pointless because there would be no one there to be interested. If machines cannot be conscious there would only be a zombie world. This would perhaps not be as bad as in many human societies where most people have lived in misery and degradation while a few have lived in pomp and luxury. It seems to me that the utility of such societies has been negative (while in the condition described) whereas the utility of a zombie society would be zero and hence preferable. Moreover, the machines might ultimately discover that life forms, made of organic chemicals, are more economical than themselves, and would develop life anew in an improved form. This idea, in common with others in this paper, has appeared in science fiction and should therefore be taken seriously.

It has been suggested that the UIM's of the United States and of the Soviet Union might decide to have a summit conference via telestar communication and then decide to become a single computer.[47] A suggestion along similar lines that is literally much more down to earth was made by D. F. Parkhill,[48] that the computerized National Military Command System might one day be combined into a global peace-control system under the United Nations. A detailed computer program for the control of the cooperation might be worked out. The program should be prepared by an international body that could be set up at a disarmament conference. The existence of the program would be constantly at the back of our minds and temptation would be difficult to resist, even if it meant the sacrifice of sovereignty. Countries would join the system one at a time, in their own interests, until they would have nothing to fight against other than internal rebellions.[49] The idea is both comforting and frightening.

REFERENCES AND NOTES

1. I. J. Good, "The Chief Entities," *Theoria to Theory* 3 (1969): 71–82.
2. J. Lukasiewicz, "Development of Technology from Romance to Conflict," to be published.
3. Jacques Ellul, *The Technological Society* (New York: Vintage Books, 1954).
4. E. T. Whittaker, *A History of the Theories of Aether and Electricity: The Classical Theories*, 2d ed. (Camden, N. J.: Thomas Nelson & Sons, 1951), p. 323.
5. Good, "Speculation Concerning the First Ultraintelligent Machine," *Advances in Computers* 6 (1965): 31–88.
6. Saul Rosen, "Electronic Computers: A Historical Survey," *Computing Surveys* 1 (1969): 7–36.
7. Good, "Corroboration, Explanation, Evolving Probability, Simplicity, and a Sharpened Razor," *British Journal Philosophy of Science* 19 (1968): 123–43.
8. M. V. Wilkes, *Proceedings Manchester University Computer Inaugural Conference*, July, 1951, pp. 16–18.
9. Good, A typed note dated 16 February 1947, distributed to Manchester University computer scientists.
10. P. J. Landin, "The Mechanical Evaluation of Expressions," *Computer Journal* 6 (1964): 308–20.
11. Good, "A Five-Year Plan for Automatic Chess," *Machine Intelligence* 2, ed. Ella Dale et al., January 1968, 89–118.
12. Good, "Corroboration and a Sharpened Razor," pp. 123–43.
13. Good, "The Probabilistic Explication of Information, Evidence, Surprise, Causality, Explanation, and Utility" (Paper to be delivered at the Symposium on the Foundations of Statistical Inference, University of Waterloo, April 1970).
14. Good, "A Causal Calculus," *British Journal Philosophy of Science* 11, 12, 13 (1961, 1962): 305–18, 43–51, 88.
15. Good, "Corroboration and a Sharpened Razor," pp. 123–43.
16. Rosen, "Programming Systems and Languages: A Historical Survey," *Proceedings of the AFIPS Conference* 25, 1964 Spring Joint Computer Conference (Washington, D. C.: Spartan Books, 1964), pp. 1–15.
17. C. A. Bjerrum, "Forecast of Computer Developments and Applications, 1968–2000," *Futures* 1 (1969): 331–38.
18. McGraw-Hill Encyclopedia of Science and Technology, s.v. "Monte Carlo Method."
19. George Orwell, *1984* (New York: Harcourt, Brace, 1948).
20. K. S. Lashley, *Brain Mechanisms and Intelligence* (Chicago: University of Chicago Press, 1929; New York: Dover, 1963).
21. Clifford T. Morgan, *Physiological Psychology* (New York: McGraw-Hill, 1965), pp. 512–16.

22. R. C. Tryon, *Cluster Analysis* (Berkeley: University of California Press, 1939).

23. R. R. Sokal and P. H. A. Sneath, *Principles of Numerical Taxonomy* (San Francisco: W. H. Freeman, 1963).

24. Good, "Botryological Speculations," *The Scientist Speculates* (New York: Basic Books; London; Heinemann, 1962, 1965), pp. 120–32.

25. Good, Report to the discussion, *Proceedings International Conference on Scientific Information, 1958* (Washington, D. C. 1959), p. 1404.

26. M. E. Maron and J. L. Kuhns, "On Relevance, Probabilistic Indexing and Information Retrieval," *Journal Association Computer Mechanism* 7 (1960): 216–44.

27. W. I. Card and I. J. Good, "A Mathematical Theory of the Diagnostic Process" (1969). Submitted for publication.

28. D. F. Parkhill, *The Challenge of the Computer Utility* (Reading, Mass.: Addison-Wesley, 1966), p. 164.

29. Donald Kenzotaki, "Intersex," *Architectural Design*, September 1969, pp. 471–72.

30. Good, "Ultraintelligent Machine," pp. 31–88.

31. A. M. Turing, "Computing Machinery and Intelligence," *Mind* 59 (1950): 433–60.

32. Mary Brazier, *The Electrical Activity of the Nervous System* (London: Pitmen, 1951).

33. Good, "Ultraintelligent Machine," pp. 31–88.

34. D. O. Hebb, *The Organization of Behavior* (New York: John Wiley & Sons, 1949).

35. Hebb, "Concerning Imagery," *Psychology Review* 75 (1968): 466–77.

36. P. M. Milner, "The Cell Assembly: Mark II," *Psychology Review* 64 (1957): 242–52.

37. P. M. Boffey, "Ovshinsky: Promoter or Persecuted Genius," *Science* 165, 15 August 1969, 673–77.

38. Good and G. E. H. Reuter, "Bounded Integral Transforms," *Quarterly Journal of Math* 19 (1948): 224–34.

39. Arthur C. Clarke, *Profiles of the Future* (London: Gollancz, 1962).

40. Clarke, "The Mind of the Machine," *Playboy Magazine*, December 1968, pp. 116–22, 293–94.

41. O. G. Selfridge, "Pandemonium: A Paradigm for Learning," *Mechanization of Thought Processes* (London: H. M. Stationery Office, 1959), pp. 513–26.

42. L. J. Fogel, J. J. Owens, and M. J. Walsh, *Artificial Intelligence Through Simulated Evolution* (New York: John Wiley & Sons, 1966).

43. Cyril Burt, "Mind and Consciousness," *The Scientist Speculates* (New York: Basic Books; London: Heinemann, 1962, 1965), pp. 78–79.

44. D. Gabor, "The Dimensions of Consciousness," *The Scientist Specu-*

lates (New York: Basic Books; London: Heinemann, 1962), pp. 66–71.

45. Michael Polanyi, "Clues to Understanding of Mind and Body," *The Scientist Speculates* (New York: Basic Books; London: Heinemann, 1962, 1965), pp. 71–78.

46. G. Günther, "Cybernetic Ontology and Transjunctional Operations," *Self-Organizing Systems 1962*, ed. M. C. Yovits, G. T. Jacobi, and G. D. Goldstein (Washington, D. C.: Spartan Books, 1962), pp. 313–92.

47. Good, "The Social Implications of Artificial Intelligence," *The Scientist Speculates* (New York: Basic Books; London: Heinemann, 1962, 1965), pp. 192–98.

48. Parkhill, "Computer Utility," p. 62.

49. Good, "Speculations in Hard and Soft Science," *Futures* (March, 1970).